Outdoor Plants for Indoor Rooms

Outdoor Plants for Indoor Rooms

Kathy Sheldon

LARK BOOKS

A Division of Sterling Publishing Co., Inc.
New York

Art Director:
Tom Metcalf

Production:
Tom Metcalf

Cover Design:
Barbara Zaretsky

Photography:
Evan Bracken
Sandy Stambaugh

Illustrations:
Stacy Gray
Orrin Lundgren

Production Assistance:
Hannes Charen

Library of Congress Cataloging-in-Publication Data

Sheldon, Kathy, 1959
    Outdoor plants for indoor rooms / by Kathy Sheldon.
      p. cm.
    ISBN 1-57990-239-1 (hardcover) 1-57990-389-4 (paperback)
    1. Indoor gardening. 2. Container gardening. 3. House plants.
    4. Plants, Ornamental. I.Title.

SB419 .S475 2001
635.9'65–dc21
                                                          CIP
                                                    2001029470

    10 9 8 7 6 5 4 3 2 1

Published by Lark Books, a division of
Sterling Publishing Co., Inc.
387 Park Avenue South, New York, N.Y. 10016

First Paperback Edition 2002
© 2001, Lark Books

Distributed in Canada by Sterling Publishing,
c/o Canadian Manda Group, One Atlantic Ave., Suite 105
Toronto, Ontario, Canada M6K 3E7

Distributed in the U.K. by Guild of Master Craftsman Publications Ltd.,
Castle Place, 166 High Street, Lewes, East Sussex, England BN7 1XU
Tel: (+ 44) 1273 477374, Fax: (+ 44) 1273 478606, Email:
pubs@thegmcgroup.com, Web: www.gmcpublications.com

Distributed in Australia by Capricorn Link (Australia) Pty Ltd.,
P.O. Box 704, Windsor, NSW 2756, Australia

If you have questions or comments about this book, please contact:
Lark Books
67 Broadway
Asheville, NC 28801
(828) 236-9730

Printed in China

ISBN 1-57990-239-1 (hardcover) 1-57990-389-4 (paperback)

Contents

6 Introduction

10 Indoor gardening basics

38 Decorating with plants

56 Room-by-room gardens

126 Botanical names

127 Acknowledgments

128 Index

Introduction

Most of us love to have living plants or flowers in our homes, but we've grown tired of the same old philodendron in a plastic pot or we feel we lack the artistry of a floral designer to make cut flowers come to life. This book will introduce you to a whole new category of plants you can use to decorate your home— outdoor plants. It's an exciting concept that allows you to bring your garden indoors for a fresh, contemporary look. Often lower in cost than a bouquet of flowers, outdoor plants in attractive containers can fill your living space with an array of colors, scents, and forms. In place of a spider plant in a macramé holder, you can have exotic flowering vines, curly-tipped grasses, and bulbs bursting with spring fragrance to enhance every room of your home.

But perhaps you're confused by the phrase *outdoor plant;* it is,

after all, a redundant term when you stop to consider the fact that every plant grows outdoors somewhere. Conventional houseplants are, for the most part, tropical plants that are found in the shade beneath the jungle canopy in nature. They've become houseplants because they can survive beneath the shady canopy of your roof. Outdoor plants, on the other hand, are plants that are more typically grown out in the garden or perhaps in a container on the patio. They're used to sun and a certain amount of cold weather. In some cases these plants will last indoors for only a couple of weeks, but in other cases they can grow inside for months or even indefinitely. Unlike cut flowers, which get tossed after about a week in the vase, many of these plants can be planted outside or grown in a pot on your patio once they've had their fill of indoor living. The pansies on the previous page are actually still in flats;

it took ten minutes to set them on the table and then cover the plastic trays with bagged moss.

To help you keep outdoor plants thriving indoors for as long as possible, the first chapter of the book will explain how to meet plant needs in your home. Along with examining light, water, soil, food, and humidity needs, this section will also show you how to pot plants (or in many cases get away *without* having to pot them!), how to purchase healthy plants, bring plants in from the garden, coax bulbs to bloom in the middle of winter, and both prevent and remedy pests and diseases.

Perhaps you already have a green thumb, but you feel like you're all thumbs when it comes to decorating your home. Then turn to the next chapter. It offers information, ideas, and inspiration to help you get the look you're after. You'll learn to use a plant's color, size, form, and texture to enhance your home, whether you live in a Colonial in the country or an urban loft.

Once you become hooked on bringing outdoor plants indoors, you'll discover that a well-rounded collection of containers is the key to both keeping plants healthy and to using plants to beautify your rooms quickly. The section on containers shows you how to acquire just such a collection, without breaking your budget. Stores have an overwhelming amount of plant containers to choose from, but you may be surprised to find that your own attic, kitchen, or local flea market is also brimming with possible plant holders.

After that, you'll find page after page of plants—some single specimens, some table-top gardens—growing indoors. There's something for everyone here. If you'd like an exotic flowering vine that produces edible fruit and can grow indoors year-round, check out the passionflower on page 90. If the thought of another dreary winter has you down, turn to page 88 to see just how cheerful a basket of spring bulbs can be in February! Perhaps you've got guests coming for dinner tonight and you'd like something special for the table. Stop by the garden center and pick up a few potted plants on

your way home from the supermarket (you may even find plants *at* your supermarket), and then just pop them into a container when you get home. Arrange a bit of moss to hide the plastic pots, and in a matter of minutes you've got a centerpiece, like the one on page 74, that looks as if you've been carefully cultivating it for weeks!

Once you widen your view of what qualifies as an indoor plant and what works as a plant holder, you'll see that the list of plants and containers you can use to decorate your home is endless. And, by the way, you don't need to throw out that cherished spider plant (although you may want to consider replacing the macramé hanger). Look carefully at our collection, and you'll see that we've sometimes given conventional houseplants a new look just by combining them with outdoor plants. Don't be afraid to break a few rules here; after all, many of your creations will be, like the perfect petals of a flower, only a fleeting pleasure. But what an exquisite pleasure they can bring.

Water

Soil

Indoor gardening
basics

Potting

Light

they can't jump out of the soil to stalk prey or lean over and munch on a neighbor. Instead, as you'll recall from science class, they use light to produce sugar and starches in a process called *photosynthesis*. Meeting light requirements is the factor that most limits which outdoor plants will be happy indoors. Even plants that will be guests in your home for only a couple of weeks will look their best if you can meet their light needs.

Amount and Intensity of Light

A plant's light requirements can be broken down into two separate components: *amount* and *intensity*. The amount of light preferred is simply the number of hours of light the plant should receive each day. Some plants, called long-day plants, need many hours of daylight to bloom. Short-day plants, on the other hand, require a certain number of hours of darkness to bloom. Luckily, most plants are not too particular about the exact number of hours of light required. The second (and in most cases, more important) component, the intensity of light needed, describes how bright the light should

The Indoor Gardener

When you turn an outdoor plant into a houseplant, even for a short spell, you make that plant entirely dependent on you for its needs. Meeting those needs is usually not very difficult or even time-consuming, but it *is* easier if you have an understanding of the basics of indoor plant care. We'll start with the requirement that has the biggest impact on indoor plant health—light.

Light

Plants need light to live; it's as simple as that. Like all living things, plants must eat, but be. Some plants—and this includes many of the flowering plants we grow in our gardens—want full, direct sun. Plants that have traditionally been used as houseplants often can't tolerate direct sun and prefer shadier conditions.

The light requirements of the plants in this book fall into one of the following four categories:

Direct Sun (sunlight actually falls on the plant's leaves). These plants generally need to be placed within 2 feet (61 cm) of a south-facing window. They may need light shade (from a sheer curtain or blind) at midday in summer.

Some Direct Sun. These plants do well within 2 feet (61 cm) of an east- or west-facing window or close to but more than 2 feet (61 cm) away from a south-facing window.

Bright Light (sun rays don't actually touch the plant). These plants need to be within 5 feet (1.5 m) of a sunny window, but not in a position where sunlight actually falls on their leaves. They may also do well close to a large sunless window.

Semishade. These plants should be 5 to 8 feet (1.5 to 2.5 m) from a sunny window or closer to a sunless window.

Plant tags, knowledgeable nursery workers, and plant encyclopedias are all good sources of information about a specific plant's light needs. But figuring out what an individual plant requires is only half the battle; next you need to determine how to meet those needs inside your house.

Indoor Light

If you're looking about your house and you don't see a lot of sunlight, don't throw in the trowel and stick plastic plants in your windowsills yet. Remember, many of the plants in this book are meant to be out in the garden, not in the house, so your goal is to get them to last a little longer than, say, a bouquet of the same cost. Most plants can survive a temporary stay in less-than-ideal light conditions. There's no reason you can't move a sun-loving flowering plant to a bedside table in a north-facing guest room for a couple of days. And a plant that prefers semishade can spend a few hours as the centerpiece in a sunny dining room for Sunday brunch (just don't set such a plant in hot,

direct light). But some garden plants will last indoors for weeks, months, or even indefinitely. For these plants, the orientation of your rooms and, more to the point, the orientation of the windows in those rooms will determine where they can be placed.

Southern Windows. These will have the brightest light and will have full, direct sun for the longest period of the day. This makes southern windows the hottest (and driest) spot for plants. In general, this is the best location for meeting the light requirements of plants that need direct light. But be careful—the intensity of the southern sun will burn many plants. It may be necessary, especially in summer, to hang up a sheer curtain to provide some relief. Plants that need bright, but not direct, light

can often grow a few feet farther into the room from a southern window.

West-facing Windows. These windows receive direct light in the afternoon, when the sun is at its hottest. That means any plants placed here must be able to tolerate intense heat and generally dry conditions, especially in the summer.

East-facing Windows. These windows will receive bright, direct morning sun, which is the coolest sun of the day, and then indirect sun in the afternoon. This makes it the ideal spot for many plants, especially those that require some direct sun, but would be harmed by the excess sun of a southern window or the heat of a western one.

North-facing Windows. These windows receive only indirect light and are the coolest locations for plants. Very few flowering plants will do well in this location, but many foliage plants would be happy here.

Further Considerations

To the human eye, the levels of light intensity may not seem to vary much from spot to spot within a room. But light intensity actually increases and decreases quite significantly as you move close to or away from a window. Remember that a few feet can make a considerable difference when it comes to finding the ideal location for your plants' light needs.

The time of year is also important. Sunlight will be less intense in winter than in summer. Plants that are happy by a northern window in summer may need to be close to a southern window during the winter months. Other factors can also affect the amount of light in a room. Obstructions such as trees, roof overhangs, and even dirty glass can block sunlight from getting into a room. The size of the window and the colors of both the inside and the outside of your house will also influence the amount of sunlight available to your plants.

And finally, get in the habit of turning plant containers one-quarter turn, always in the same direction, every few weeks to ensure even growth; otherwise, your plants will begin to lean toward the light. Do not turn plants with buds just about to bloom, however, or they may refuse to open.

The following are signs that your plants are receiving too much light:

- Leaves are sunburned (look for brown or gray scorched spots)

- Leaves dry up and drop off

- Leaves wilt at midday

- Leaves look dull

The following are signs that your plants need more light:

- Leaves turn yellow and drop off

- Leaves are smaller than normal

- Plant has spindly growth

- Plant isn't blooming well

- Variegated leaves turn solid green

Water

Everyone's heard that you'll kill a goldfish by overfeeding it and you'll kill a houseplant if you overwater it, but plants need water just like fish need food, so how do you decide how much is enough? Well, it *can* be tricky, but like so many other things in life, it's mostly a matter of practice. Plants, like humans, are composed mostly of water, and that water must be constantly replenished. If it isn't, the plant will eventually die. But plants also need oxygen, and they get that oxygen from the soil through their roots. When soil is kept so wet that it doesn't hold any oxygen, then plants either asphyxiate, or they die from root rot.

You can buy all sorts of fancy gizmos to help you track the moisture content of your plants' soil, but you actually were born with the most effective one of all—your finger. Simply stick your finger into the potting soil (near the outer rim of the pot, so you don't hurt any roots) up to the first or second knuckle. This way you can feel down below the soil surface, which sometimes feels dry even though the soil below it is still moist.

Plant Types

In general, with regard to watering needs, there are four categories of plants. The first (and largest) group is made up of plants that prefer moist/dry conditions. Plants in this category need the top ½ inch (1.3 cm) of their soil to be allowed to dry out between waterings. These plants also typically need more water between spring and autumn, when they are actively growing, and less in winter, when they're resting.

The second group of plants prefers evenly moist soil. Lots of flowering plants belong to this group. It's important, though, not to confuse *moist* with *wet*: water whenever the soil surface becomes dry, but don't keep the soil saturated. Many plants in this group also need less water in winter.

Drought-tolerant plants make up the third group. Most of these plants need to be watered in the same manner as moist/dry plants when they're actively growing. But in winter their roots are extremely sensitive to excess moisture, and their soil should be allowed to dry out almost completely.

The fourth (and fairly small) group of plants consists of those that need constantly wet soil in order to survive. As you might suppose, these are plants that are found in the same conditions in nature.

As with light requirements, the water needs of a specific plant can be determined from plant tags, knowledgeable nursery workers, or a plant encyclopedia. But remember to take into account that most of the plants in this book are intended for outdoor gardens. Because you'll be growing the plant in a container indoors (where, for instance, the air in winter can be very dry), you may need to adjust the actual amount of water the plant receives.

How to Water

When watering, it's important to remember that, with plants, what you don't see is as important as what you do see. Try to imagine yourself as a plant. You'd be upside down with your head and chest stuck into the soil, and your legs and feet sticking up in the air. Beginning gardeners sometimes make the mistake of watering a plant's leaves, when it's the roots down below the soil that are thirsty. And remember, you want those roots to grow deep, so the plant stays healthy. If you dribble just a bit of water on the soil surface every day or two, the roots will need to stay up near that surface in order to get a drink. If you instead water only when the plant needs it and then water deeply, the roots will extend down into the soil to create a stabler, healthier plant.

Plants can be watered from the top or from the bottom. To water from the top, simply pour tepid tap water (cold water can shock plants and spot the leaves) onto the soil surface in a steady stream until you see water start to pour out of the pot's drainage hole. Empty any water still remaining in the pot's saucer after half an hour. Some plants have delicate leaves and stems that can be damaged from overhead watering, and these are best watered from below. To do so, fill the saucer with tepid tap water and wait while the water is sucked up through the dry soil in the pot. If all of the water is wicked up quickly, add a bit more. The surface of the potting soil should be moist after a half hour or so. Once the surface is moist, empty any water left in the saucer.

Watering Groups of Plants

You've probably noticed, if you've thumbed through this book, that in many cases more than one plant is sharing a pot. Does that mean that you can grow only plants with the same watering needs together? That depends. If you're planting the plants right into the pot, all in the same soil, then they will need to all have similar water requirements. But if you cheat and instead keep each individual plant in its own pot, and then· slip those pots into a larger container (usually the smaller pots inside the container are hidden with moss of some type), you can combine plants with different water needs. (See page 26 for more on the different methods of potting plants.)

When to Water

It may seem that establishing a regular routine to water all your plants, say, every Saturday morning would keep them happy and healthy. Instead, though, it might kill them. Not only do different plants have different water needs, but an individual plant's water needs may change. What follows are some of the key factors, aside from plant type, that affect the water needs of a plant.

Time of Year. In summer, when most plants are actively growing and the air is warm, plants need to be watered more often. In winter, many plants are dormant and the sun is less intense; these plants should then be watered less often, typically only one to three times a month.

Location. Plants near windows facing south or west are apt to dry out quickly. The closer to the window the plant is set, the faster it will dry out (and the more water it will need), since light levels are most intense directly in front of a window and then drop as you go farther into the room.

Room's Temperature and Humidity. Indoor gardeners who keep their thermostats set high in the winter need to water their plants more often. If you bundle up and keep the temperature in your home on the cool side (about 65°F [18°C]), most of your plants will be happier and will need less water. Taking care of your plants' humidity needs (see page 21) will mean that they'll need less water.

Plant and Pot Size. In general, plant size affects water needs in a straightforward manner: bigger plants have bigger rootballs and therefore need more water. (Exceptions, of course, would be large drought-tolerant plants, such as cacti.) When a plant becomes so large that its roots take up most of the pot, leaving little room for soil to hold moisture, it will need to be watered more often. But don't make the mistake of repotting into a much larger pot, thinking it will save you trips with the watering can—plants are happiest when you move up only one pot size at each repotting.

Container Type. The type of container you use will also affect the amount of watering needed. Pots made from a porous material, such as terra cotta, absorb water and allow the soil to dry out sooner than plastic or other nonporous containers. However, since it's easy to kill a plant by overwatering it, plastic containers should be used with caution.

The following are signs that a plant is underwatered:

•Limp, wilted leaves

•Little or no new leaf growth

•Oldest leaves fall; then others

•Lower leaves curl, yellow, and wilt

•Flowers fade quickly or fall

The following are signs that a plant is overwatered:

•New and old leaves drop

•Leaves are limp

•Brown leaf tips

•Leaves curl, yellow, and wilt

Temperature

Usually, plants inside your home will be happy if daytime temperatures are in the 60 to 75°F (15 to 23°C) range. At night, most plants prefer cooler temperatures and are content with a range between 60 and 65°F (15 and 18°C). This daily variation between day and night temperatures is important to the health of many plants.

Of course, plants do vary in their temperature needs. Some will refuse to bloom unless they get a certain number of cool nights. Others are so sensitive to the cold that they'll die very quickly in temperatures below 50°F (10°C). But a wide variety of plants can tolerate temperatures slightly above or below their ideal range for a short period of time.

Indoor Temperatures

It may seem that our modern homes, equipped with furnaces and air conditioners, would be the ideal place to meet a plant's temperature needs—simply set the thermostat to stay within the preferred range of day and night temperatures. But it's a bit more complicated than that. Your house, if you think about it, is a collection of microclimates, and temperatures can vary widely, not just throughout the house, but also within a single room. Windows, where we tend to place plants for sunlight, can be especially problematic. The sun streaming through a window on a warm summer day can cook a plant. (Moving plants slightly farther into the room may help, as will opening the window or hanging a sheer curtain.) Placing a plant close to a window can be equally dangerous in winter. If the leaves come in contact with the glass, which conducts cold, they can easily freeze.

Winter is also a time to watch out for plants placed too close to radiators and heat vents. Many older homes have radiators with shelves above them that are the perfect spot for plants in warm weather. But in winter you must make sure the plants won't get too hot. Another indoor microclimate you may not have considered is the space hanging plants occupy, up near the ceiling. Since heat rises, conditions there will be warmer (and drier) than in the rest of the room. And finally, plants don't appreciate cold drafts any more than humans do. Keep them away from air conditioners (which will also dry them out quickly) and out of drafty entryways in winter.

Humidity and Air

Humidity is one of the less obvious factors that can have a real impact on how well plants thrive inside your home. Turn the air conditioner on in summer or the heat up in winter and the air can become extremely dry; in many homes the air in winter is literally as dry as that of a desert! You may notice your own skin become dry and itchy, but neglect to notice how your plants are suffering. If your plants seem to be distressed from lack of humidity, try the following remedies.

Misting. This is a low-tech but effective way to combat dry conditions. Forget about those tiny brass misters that are adorable but require countless trips to the kitchen sink. Use a decent size spray bottle (an inexpensive plastic one is fine) to cover your plants with a light mist. Use tepid, not cold, water, and spray plants out of direct light. It's best to mist in the morning, so the foliage has a chance to dry before evening. Certain plants with soft or hairy leaves, such as begonias and gloxinias, should not be misted since the water can damage their foliage.

Grouping Plants. Plants generate their own humidity as the leaves release water vapor. When you cluster plants together, you create a sort of jungle effect that can help raise the humidity level for the plants. Just be sure that the plants aren't so close together that air circulation is compromised.

Pebble Trays. If you set your plants on a shallow tray filled with pebbles and water, evaporating moisture will rise up and increase the humidity levels near the plant's foliage. Just about any kind of saucer that holds water should work fine. Simply add a 1 to 2-inch (2.5 to 5 cm) layer of pebbles or gravel and enough water to

reach just below the tops of the pebbles. Then place your potted plants down on the pebbles, making sure the water level isn't high enough to touch the bottoms of the pots.

Too Much Humidity

It *is* possible for a plant to suffer from excessive humidity. This is most likely to happen when you place a plant that prefers drier air in a location such as a greenhouse (or perhaps a bathroom) that has high humidity and poor air circulation. If you notice a plant suffering from the symptoms listed below, try moving it to a drier place in your home, or take the steps recommended in the following section to improve air circulation.

Air

Plants also need fresh air and adequate air circulation to stay free of pests and diseases. Don't crowd plants too closely together, and let fresh air into your home whenever possible; open a window a crack in winter if it warms up a bit outside. Just don't let a cold draft blow directly onto a plant. You can also use a fan to help move air about a room, but again, don't let it blow directly onto a plant.

The following are signs that a plant needs more humidity:

•Flowers shrivel up and fall off

•Tips of leaves shrivel and turn brown

•Edges of leaves turn yellow, may wilt

The following are signs that a plant needs less humidity:

•Flowers and leaves get moldy

•Leaves and stems rot

Soil

Outdoor gardeners know that the secret to a great garden is great garden soil. The soil must provide the plants with a home where they can stretch out their roots, quench their thirst, take in needed nutrients, and breathe in oxygen. Indoors, all that must be accomplished by soil confined to a container. This soil must be able to retain the water and nutrients necessary for plant health while allowing for adequate drainage and root growth. Until fairly recently, indoor gardeners had the time-consuming and messy task of mixing their own potting soil. But nowadays, premium potting soils are bagged and waiting for you at your local nursery or garden center.

Many of these potting soils actually contain no soil at all. Instead they're made up of a combination of ingredients that make a lightweight, porous, and clean growing medium. Most nurseries now grow their plants (and sell them) in soilless composts, so you'll put less stress on newly purchased plants if you pot them in soilless mixes. But there are some disadvantages to soilless mixes. Those that contain peat moss are very difficult to water if they're ever allowed to dry out completely. They're also so light that potted plants can become top-heavy and tip over easily (adding a layer of sand to the surface of the mix after potting can help remedy this).

For outdoors plants that will be houseplants only temporarily, just about any good potting soil should suffice. (Look out for bags that are very heavy or don't list the ingredients—a few manufacturers are still trying to pass plain old dirt off as potting soil.) If you're planning to grow a plant, such as the passion vine, that can live indoors indefinitely, then ask a knowledgeable nursery worker to recommend the best mix for that particular plant.

Whatever you do, don't use soil from your garden. It's apt to contain pests, diseases, and weed seeds, and it will drain poorly. You'll wind up with a pot of rock-hard dirt and dead plants.

spread out in search of nutrients. In a pot, of course, the roots have only so far to go, and the potting soil contains a limited amount of nutrition that doesn't naturally replenish itself. Each time you water your plants, some of the food in the potting soil is taken up by the plant roots and some of it leaches out of the container's drain hole. Within a couple of months, all the food in the soil will be depleted; after that, your plants will depend on you to give them fertilizer to provide the food they need.

When to Fertilize

Before you start preparing a feast for your plants, wait! It's important to remember that only *actively growing* plants need food, and most plants have a period of dormancy (usually winter) when they stop growing and rest. With the exception of winter-blooming plants, most need little or no fertilizer in the fall and winter months.

Kinds of Fertilizer

Fertilizers come in various forms: liquid, powder, granules, and sticks. Fast-acting, water-soluble fertilizers (liquids and powders) tend to be the most effective way to feed

Feeding

Although plants can produce sugars through a process called photosynthesis, they still need other substances—in particular, nitrogen, phosphorus, and potassium—when they're actively growing. In nature this food comes from organic material in the soil. Every time it rains, plant roots (which can only take in food that is in a liquid state) suck up a "power drink" of nutrients from the ground. In ideal conditions the organic material in soil constantly replenishes itself, and even when the soil is less fertile, the plant roots can plants indoors, since they reach the roots almost immediately. The easiest way to use this type is to add a small amount (less than the manufacturer's recommendation) to the water every other time you water your plants during their active growing season.

Granular fertilizers that are placed on the soil surface and sticks you push into the soil (these are slow-release fertilizers) are convenient but typically less effective than the fast-acting types. It's more difficult for these types to get the nutrients deep into the soil (which is necessary for proper root development). Also, there's a good chance with these slow-release methods that the fertilizer will still be in the soil when the plant is dormant and can be harmed from too much food. In fact, over-fertilization can occur even when plants are actively growing, and it will harm your plants. Resist the temptation to treat your plants to an extra dose of fertilizer. Instead of making them even bigger and stronger, it will stunt their growth and burn their leaves.

The following are signs of under-fertilization:

•No blooms or small flowers

•Slow growth

•Leaves are pale

•Stems are weak

The following are signs of over-fertilization:

•Weak, stunted growth

•Leaves have brown spots and scorched edges

•White crust on pot from salt accumulation

Potting Plants

Perhaps like many people you suffer from pot-aphobia. Potting a plant seems like such a messy and complicated process that you sometimes just leave your plants sitting in their (gasp) tacky plastic grow pots. Well, fear not. First of all, most of the potting soils sold these days are carefully formulated to eliminate problems such as poor drainage that plagued container gardeners in the past. And second of all, keep in mind that many of the plants in this book are going to be sitting in their container in your house for a matter of weeks, not months, so you don't need to provide them with five-star accommodations.

Single Plant in a Container

Follow these steps if you're potting a single plant into a container.

1. Water the plant thoroughly (preferably an hour or two before potting it).

2. Clean previously used pots by soaking them in a solution of one part chlorine bleach to nine parts water, and then rinse them well. (Terra-cotta pots need to be soaked in water for several hours before potting plants into them, or their porous sides will wick away the soil's moisture.)

3. Place a thin layer of clay shards (broken pieces of terra-cotta pots) or gravel over the drainage hole. You can add a bit of horticultural charcoal over this to help keep the potting soil sweet.

4. Remove the plant from its nursery pot by placing your hand over the top of the pot with the stem between your fingers (as shown in figure 1). Turn the pot upside down; then pull the pot away from the plant (not the other way around). If the pot doesn't slip off, tap the pot against a hard surface and try again. If the pot still refuses to budge after several taps, you may need to run a knife blade around the inside of the pot or snip the pot with scissors and tear it apart.

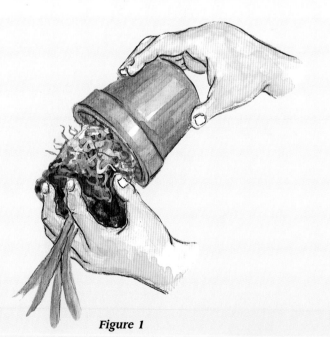

Figure 1

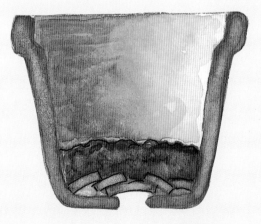

Figure 2

5. Gently tease out any matted or tangled roots from the plant's root ball.

6. Pour just enough potting soil into the bottom of the pot so the plant will sit at the same level that it sat in its nursery pot (see figure 2).

7. Center the plant in the pot, and then add potting soil around the edges until the top of the soil is ½ inch (1.3 cm) below the rim of the pot (any higher and you'll have messy overflows when you water indoors). Press down gently on the soil surface to eliminate air pockets (as shown in figure 3).

8. Water the plant thoroughly, and keep it out of direct light for several days.

Multiple Plants in a Container

Follow these steps to plant several plants in a single large container.

1. Follow steps 1 through 3 for potting single plants; then pour enough soil into the container to fill it almost full. Firm the soil.

2. Starting with the container's most central plant (typically, the largest), dig a hole in the potting soil to match the size of the plant's nursery pot. Insert the plant, pot and all, into the hole (as shown in figure 4) to check for fit, and add or take away soil as needed (the plant should sit in the soil at the same level it sits in its nursery pot).

3. Follow steps 4 and 5 for potting a single plant (on pages 26 and 27) to remove the pot from the plant and gently tease out tangled roots.

4. Set the plant in the hole and gently firm the soil around it.

5. Plant the rest of the plants in the same manner, working your way out from the center to the edges of the container.

Figure 3

Figure 4

Buying Plants

With gardening's surge in popularity, it sometimes seems as if, spring through fall, you can barely turn around without bumping into a plant for sale. Go to the grocery store to buy a quart of milk, and a potted primrose beckons; stop at one of those large home-improvement stores for a screwdriver, and a humongous garden center with flats upon flats of flowers is there to tempt you. So how do you decide first where to buy your plants and then what to look for when you make a purchase? A safe rule-of-thumb would be to find a local nursery with a knowledgeable staff and only buy plants there. Such places are usually scrupulous about.

taking care of their plants, throwing out unhealthy plants fast (after all, they can't afford to lose their entire inventory to pests or disease), and providing you with detailed information about each plant's cultural needs.

However, if you shop at nurseries only, you will pass up some opportunities to buy perfectly fine plants at a bargain. This is because, while nurseries often do have better quality plants for sale, sometimes the plants at the grocery store, discount department store, home-improvement center, florist shop, and nursery all came from the same supplier. The difference is the treatment they receive (or don't receive) once they get to the stores. If you're smart, you'll befriend a clerk or manager at one of those other stores and find out when a new truckload of plants is due. If you can purchase plants within a day or two of their arrival, the store won't have time to let them dry out or become infested with bugs.

Wherever you shop, search out the healthiest looking plants. When you find a plant that looks good, pick it up. If the plant and its pot feel sur-

Here's what you want to see when you look at a plant you're considering for purchase:

•A plant tag with care instructions. (Unless you already know this plant's needs or can find a staffer who does, you're taking a chance on being able to grow it in your home.)

•Solid, firm stems

•Uniformly spaced, bright green leaves (evidence of new leaf growth is good) with no signs of disease or insect damage

•Lots of buds (if it's a flowering plant) with just a few starting to open. (Chrysanthemums and miniature roses are exceptions to this rule; they often won't open indoors, so go ahead and buy them in full bloom.)

Here's what you don't want to see:

•Wilted leaves
•Limp, soft stems
•A plant listing to one side of the pot
•Space between the potting soil and the inside of the pot
•Almost all flowers open
•Leggy or spindly growth
•Evidence that leaves have fallen
•Yellow, brown, curled, spotted, or streaked leaves
•Leaves with insect damage

prisingly light, don't buy it. Give the pot a gentle shake. If tiny white bugs fly up, the plant is infested with whiteflies, and you don't want it. If the plant wobbles a lot, it may not be well-rooted. Take a look at the pot's drainage hole. If roots are growing out of the

hole, the plant may be rootbound, so ask to remove the plant from the pot. Don't buy the plant if its roots are wound tightly around the root ball. Finally, look under the leaves of the plant for insects and disease. Don't buy a plant with either of these problems.

Bringing Plants in from the Garden

What about bringing plants that are growing in your garden inside? This can be an inexpensive way to get non-traditional houseplants, but to do it successfully, you have to take special precautions.

First, choose a plant that's healthy; there's no point in taking a diseased or pest-infected plant and then subjecting it to the stress of transplant and a new environment. Dig the plant up, trying to get as much of the root ball as possible, and pot it into a clean container that's just a tad bigger than the root ball. Be sure to use potting soil, not garden soil; refer to page 26 for potting instructions. Next, you may need to trim back the top of the plant a bit, so it's more in balance with the size of the root ball, which is probably smaller than it was when the plant was growing in the ground. Water the plant well. Ideally, you should keep the plant outdoors in partial shade for a couple of weeks, to help it adjust to the shock of transplant.

If you're the impatient type, you can take the chance of moving the plant indoors sooner. But before you do, you absolutely must check it for insects. The natural enemies of plant pests that help to keep them in check outdoors are unavailable inside your house, and if you bring in a plant with a stowaway pest, you'll have a full-scale invasion (and dead plants) before long. If you do see a few bugs, spray the plant thoroughly with soapy water or insecticidal soap, making sure you coat both the tops and bottoms of leaves. Leave the plant in a location such as an enclosed porch, away from other plants, until you're sure it's pest-free. To be on the safe side, quarantine even those plants without any visible signs of pests for a short spell before bringing them indoors. Again, if you just have to have that begonia that's in your garden right now in a pot on your dinner table tonight, then don't skip the step of checking for bugs, and spraying if necessary.

Forcing Bulbs

As the days grow shorter and colder, the number of outdoor plants you can grow inside your home will dwindle. Winter can seem endless to plant lovers. Luckily, this is when bulbs come to the rescue. It's fascinating to watch all sort of bulbs, which look so modest in their papery tunics, burst out in brilliant display inside your home. The term *forcing* is used to describe the method of coaxing bulbs to bloom inside much sooner than they would outdoors.

It doesn't take much work (or any actual force, for that matter), but because the bulbs must be cooled for a number of weeks (to mimic the cold they would normally receive outside, under the ground), it does require some advance planning.

Check the chart on page 33 for the bulbs you'd like to grow, decide when in winter you want them to bloom, and then count back to find the date you'll need to start cooling them. When you purchase your bulbs, buy the best you can afford and make sure they're large and firm with no soft spots or mold. The nursery or mail-order company selling bulbs should be able to recommend cultivars for forcing.

To prepare bulbs for forcing, you'll need a clean plastic or terra-cotta pot or a bulb pan with a drainage hole. (It's a good idea to soak terra-cotta pots overnight in the tub first so they don't absorb all the potting soil's moisture.) Bulb pans, which are wide and low, often work better than taller, narrower pots that can tip over

once the plants grow tall. First, place a layer of gravel on the bottom of the container, then add in loose potting soil that drains easily (you can mix a little sand in with the soil to help with drainage). Plant bulbs close together, but not so close that they touch one another or the sides of the pot. Plant so that their tops (the pointy tip) is even with the top edge of the container. Because different types of bulbs will bloom at different times, it's safest to plant only one type per pot. This still leaves you with the option of using different bulbs that bloom at the same time to make a lovely arrangement in a large basket or other container serving as a cachepot.

Water the pot well and label it with the bulb type and the planting date. Now the bulbs must be stored in a dark, cold—between 40 and 50°F (4 and 10°C)—location. Try a corner of an unheated basement or garage, a back porch, or a basement window well. The potted bulbs can also be buried in a trench in the ground under a thick layer of straw to keep them from freezing. Wherever you store them, take precautions to make sure that mice, squirrels, and raccoons can't eat them and that they won't

freeze. Check the pots weekly to make certain the soil is moist but not wet. Bulbs can also be stored in a refrigerator as long as it doesn't contain fruit, which emits ethylene gas that will ruin the bulbs' flowers.

After the required amount of time has passed (see the chart on the facing page), check the pot's drainage hole to see if roots are developing. You can also carefully slip the pot away from the soil ball to check root development. Once the bulbs have produced roots that are about 2 inches (5.1 cm) long, set the container in a cool room

with bright, but not direct, light. The bulbs should bloom in a few weeks. During flowering, keep the plants cool (especially at night), out of direct sunlight, and well watered, so they'll last as long as possible.

Water Forcing

Water forcing, a popular pastime of the Victorian Age, is an easy way to bring bulbs such as hyacinths and crocuses into bloom. Just store the bulbs in brown paper bags in a cool (50 to 55°F [10 to 12°C]) location for the required number of weeks (see chart to the right). Then place each bulb in a clear, hourglass-shaped forcing vase or in a shallow pan filled with pebbles. The water level in either container should be just high enough to touch the bottom of the bulb, but not so high that the bulb rots. Maintain this water level while storing bulbs and their container in a cool, dark location until the roots are 2 inches (5.1 cm) long (about three weeks); then place them where they'll receive bright, but not direct, light. Bulbs should bloom in about two more weeks.

Back to the Garden

Once bulbs have been forced, you won't be able to force them again, but you may be able to plant them outdoors where they should bloom again after a couple of years. If you want to try this, cut the faded blossoms, leaving the flower stalks and leaves, and continue to water and fertilize the plant until the leaves yellow and wither. Pull the entire plant, bulb and all, out of the soil and set it aside to dry for several weeks. Then remove the foliage and store the bulb in a cool dry place. Plant the bulbs outdoors in autumn. Daffodils, hyacinths, crocuses, grape hyacinths, squill, and snowdrops are all worth trying to transplant into the garden for flowers in subsequent years. Tulips, however, will rarely reward you for this effort, and should be composted once they're finished blooming.

Time Required to Cool Bulbs for Forcing

Crocus	8 to 10 weeks
Daffodil (Narcissus)	12 to 15 weeks
Hyacinth	12 to 15 weeks
Iris	10 to 14 weeks
Lily of the Valley	10 to 12 weeks
Muscari (Grape Hyacinth)	10 to 14 weeks
Scilla	10 to 12 weeks
Tulip	12 to 16 weeks

Pests and Diseases

Combating pests and diseases is one of the least pleasant aspects of growing plants indoors. But the need to do so is practically inevitable if you garden inside for any length of time. Knowing what to look for, so you can diagnose a problem and nip it in the bud before it spreads, is important. But even more important, take preventative steps to try to help keep pests and diseases from attacking your plants in the first place.

An Ounce of Prevention

•Keep plants in tip-top shape by meeting light, water, humidity, air circulation, and nutritional needs. Healthy plants are less likely to be bothered by pests and diseases (and more likely to survive an attack should one occur).

•Inspect plants carefully before bringing them into your home, whether they've come from a nursery, a friend, or your own garden. You might want to spray them with soapy water (see recipe to the right) as a precautionary measure, even if you don't see signs of pests or disease. Even better, isolate long-term plants for a couple of weeks before placing them near your other plants.

•Keep containers and the area around plants clean by picking up leaves or debris dropped by plants.

•Pots and containers that have already held plants should be sterilized before being reused. Follow the procedure on page 26.

•Once you notice a plant suffering from pests or disease, separate that plant from others and treat it immediately. You may at times need to throw out a plant rather than risk infecting others. Plants with insects or diseases should not be put in the compost pile.

A Pound of Cure

Using pesticides inside your home, where the chemical ingredients will remain in the air fair longer than you might suppose, is dangerous. There's no point in exposing yourself or your family to potentially harmful chemicals just to save a plant that probably cost less than the pesticide in the first place! If you do decide to use pesticides to treat your plants, do so outdoors and follow the label directions for applying and storing the chemicals. Sulfur sprays and powders, used for disease control, are organic fungicides (available in garden centers) that are safe for indoor use. You may want to use them outdoors also, though, since they often smell terrible. The safest alternative to pesticides is insecticidal soap you can purchase or make yourself following the simple recipe below.

Soapy Water Recipe

Add 1 tablespoon (15 mL) of mild liquid dishwashing soap to 1 gallon (3.8 L) of warm water. Pour this into a spray bottle and spray it directly onto your plants, or mix it in a bucket and gently tip the plant's foliage right into the soapy water. Leave the soapy water on the plant for two hours; then rinse the plant with warm water.

Know Your Enemies

The sooner you can determine which pest or disease is attacking your plant, the sooner you'll be able to take action and keep the problem from spreading.

Common Indoor Pests

Aphids. These are tiny sap-sucking, soft-bodied insects. They're usually green but can also be white, red, brown, black, orange, or even clear. They suck sap from soft tissues, leaving behind a sticky substance called honeydew and causing distorted growth.

Mealybugs. These are small, white insects covered with a cottony fluff. They're usually found on plant stems (where the leaves and stem join) or under leaves. Like aphids, mealybugs suck sap from plants and deposit sticky honeydew. A plant infected with mealybugs may have yellow or deformed leaves. The insects' cottony appearance makes them easy to spot.

Aphids

Remedies (Aphids)

Handpicking

Spray plants in shower (or outdoors with hose)

Spray with insecticidal soap or soapy water (see page 34)

Mealybugs

Remedies (Mealybugs)

Wipe off with a cotton ball or paper towel drenched in rubbing alcohol

Spray with soapy water (see page 34)

Scale. These are brown, oval insects that look like flat or slightly raised bumps on a plant. When mature, the insects are immobile. They suck plant juices and excrete honeydew. Their waxy coating protects them from most sprays. Plants infected with scale are sticky from the honeydew and have yellow leaves, which may fall off.

Scale

Remedies
(Scale)

Scrape by hand or with a damp cloth

Scrub off with a toothbrush dipped in soapy water

Red Spider Mites. These are tiny arachnids that suck sap from plants. They're so small that they're hard to see, but you can identify them from the delicate webbing they leave on the underside of leaves. When spider mites attack, leaves become mottled, then pale yellow, and then eventually drop off.

Remedies
(Red Spider Mites)

Spray plants in shower or outside with hose

Spray with insecticidal soap or soapy water (see page 34)

Prune heavily infested part of the plant

Red Spider Mites

Whiteflies. These are tiny, mothlike insects that cluster on the underside of leaves. When you shake the plant gently, the whiteflies will fly up and become visible. Their larvae are translucent green. They suck plant juices and excrete honeydew. When infected with whiteflies, a plant's leaves become mottled and yellow and eventually drop.

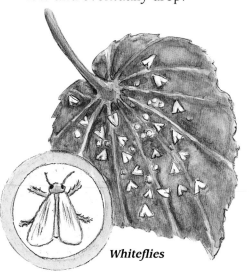

Whiteflies

Remedies (Whiteflies)

(Apply these remedies at night, when the insects are less likely to fly away.)

Wipe the undersides of leaves with a cotton ball or paper towel drenched in rubbing alcohol or soapy water

Use a hand vacuum to suck whiteflies off sturdy plants

Common Indoor Diseases

Powdery Mildew. This is a fungus that coats the surface of leaves and flowers with white or gray powdery patches. Leaves infected with powdery mildew turn yellow or brown and eventually fall off. This disease can be spread by hand, so wash well before touching uninfected parts of the plant or other plants.

Powdery Mildew

Sooty Mold. This is a black fungus that often grows in the honeydew left by sucking insects. It hinders the plant's growth by keeping sunlight from reaching the leaf surfaces.

Remedy (Powdery Mildew)

Mix 3 tablespoons (45 mL) of baking soda and 5 tablespoons (75 mL) of liquid antiseptic hand-soap into 1 gallon (3.8 mL) of warm water, and spray on plant's foliage

Remedies (Sooty Mold)

Use the remedies recommended to rid plant of pests leaving the honeydew

Wipe with damp cloth or paper towel

Spray leaves with soapy water (see page 34)

Sooty Mold

Stem and Crown Rot. This is a fungus that turns stems and roots soft and mushy. The disease attacks plants that have been overwatered or have poor drainage or air circulation.

Stem and Crown Rot

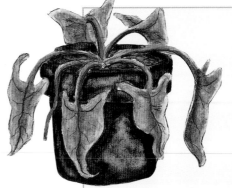

Remedy (Stem and Crown Rot)

You can try cutting away diseased parts of the plant, but you will very likely need to throw the plant away

Decorating with
plants

Here's a little game to play the next time you're thumbing through one of those home decorating magazines with sumptuous photos of to-die-for rooms. Imagine the room without the plants, cut flowers, artfully draped throws, and other special touches provided by a professional stylist. Looks kind of plain, doesn't it? Of course, a room's architecture, furniture, and wall color all play important roles in its appearance. But what those photo stylists know is that small, well-chosen details can also have an enormous impact on a room. When plants are used in this manner, they contribute design elements such as color, form, and texture, and then they go a step further. Because plants are alive, they bring a special vitality to the indoors and evoke a response that a throw pillow, however charming, is just not capable of. When the plant is not a traditional houseplant but, instead, one we're used to seeing outdoors, the effect is even stronger. Trends in decorating come and go, and even plants themselves go in and out of style, but if you trust your instincts and pay attention to just a few of the fundamentals of design, using plants to enhance your decor will come naturally.

What Most of Us Do

For most of us, much of the time, plants are an impulse purchase. You happen upon a beautiful plant in full bloom for sale, and it's hard to resist. So you buy it, bring it home, and look around hoping to find a spot where it will both look good and survive. If you're lucky, you discover the perfect location where the plant thrives while complementing the style of the room, adding the perfect accent to your decor, getting your feng shui in perfect balance, and filling your gardening friends with envy. If you're not so lucky you console yourself with the fact that you always kill plants in a matter of weeks anyway.

What We Ought to Do

The better approach, of course, is to start with the room instead of the plant. Spend some time at home (safe from the temptation of gorgeous blossoms and luscious leaves) studying each individual room, and asking yourself both what the plant needs and what you need from the plant. Decorating with living plants involves finding a balance

between horticultural and design needs. If you're using plants as temporary touches for a special occasion, and you plan to plant them outside, give them away, or toss them onto the compost pile later, then you can cheat on the plants' cultural needs (beyond keeping them temporarily presentable) and concentrate only on your decor. Otherwise, the first thing you should do is use the information in the first chapter to access each room's growing conditions.

Does your bedroom face north and receive indirect light only? Does your bathroom tend to stay humid? How far will you have to carry a watering can to get to your living room? (And if you have a tiny watering can and lots of plants, how many trips are you willing to make?) This will help you narrow your plant choices right off the bat. (You might even want to write down the growing conditions for different spots in each room and take it with you to the nursery. Then

when that bright-eyed gerber daisy gazes at you imploringly, you can show it your list and say, "Look, Bud, do you really want to roast to death in my west-facing window?")

Once you've covered the practical side of things, the fun begins. Now you can get creative and decide what a plant (or plants) could do for the room's decor. First, ask yourself what overall effect you'd like to achieve. How would you describe the style of the room? If your living room is formal, a carefully pruned topiary in a classical urn or a symetrical arrangement of plants—say, identical plants on either end of the fireplace mantle—would work well. A contemporary living room might benefit from plants with bold, interesting shapes in sleek (perhaps steel or glass) containers. In a living room with a cottage look, simple flowering plants in a rustic basket or a humble terra-cotta pot would be more in keeping with the decor. Ferns and forced bulbs could be authentic accents in a Victorian living room. Let your wall-coverings, furniture, drapes, carpet, and artwork all suggest plant selections. You may want a plant with peach-colored flowers to bring out that same color in a painting. Or it might be fun to echo the flowers found on the fabric of your throw pillows.

Plants can also solve some of your decorating problems. If you have a dark room you'd like to lighten, try plants with pale-colored flowers or variegated foliage. Plants can screen unattractive views out windows or act as room dividers. Sometimes it can be hard to figure out just what to do with an unused corner of a room—a single tall plant, or a group of plants, may be just what it needs. Once you've thought about what you'd like to improve or change in a room, you can begin to think in more detail about specific design elements, such as size and scale, shape, color, and texture.

Elements of Design

Size and Scale

First off, remember that size is always relative. It's tempting to fall into the bigger-is-better line of thinking when choosing plants to go in your home (especially if you're buying the plant in the garden section of an airplane hanger-sized home center). But place a huge cement pot of plants on a delicate table, and more than just the furniture's joints will feel stressed—when elements in a room are out of scale, humans feel uneasy. And, of course, it works the other way around, too. A delicate little violet that looks sweet on a small nightstand might easily look absurd all alone in the center of a dining room table. A row of three or even five smalls pots of violets down the center of the table could be lovely, though. Large plants will usually look best on the floor or on a low pedestal. Small and medium-size plants have the biggest impact on tables, windowsills, and shelves slightly below eye-level, while cascading plants are effective above eye-level.

Scale is also important when selecting a container for your plant. Typically, a pleasing ratio is achieved when the plant is one and one-half times the height or width of the pot. But matching container and plant size is more than a matter of aethestics—it's crucial to the plant's health. This is discussed in more detail on page 55.

Shape

Outdoor gardeners know that plant shape is often more important than color when it comes to designing a garden. This is true when gardening indoors too, whether you're considering the shape of a single plant in a pot, a group of plants in a container, or sever-al containers of plants massed together. Think of how plants can differ in their forms. Some cascade down while others scramble up, some are slim and erect, and some squat and round. A plant shaped like a tree with one central stem and side branches often works best as a single "specimen" plant. Those with bushier, mounded shapes are effective in a group. A plant with long arching stems can be beautiful in front of an arched window or mirror. One with strong, architectural lines will complement modern decor.

Don't worry, you don't need to pass a test by identifying the exact shape of each plant you want to bring into your home!

Upright

Grassy

Bushy

Trailing

Rosette

Just start paying attention to this particular aspect of design; play around a bit and you'll discover all sorts of interesting combinations and effects. After a while, noticing a plant's form will become as automatic as considering its color or size.

Along with the plant's shape, you'll also need to consider the shape of the foliage. Are the leaves small and round or long and spiky? Do they resemble narrow needles or the wide, floppy ear of an elephant? Pay attention to leaf form when combining plants and when deciding where to place them. A plant with small, intricate leaves may get lost in front of busy wallpaper. A large plant with bold, sculp-

tural leaves would work well in a room with modern decor but might look silly in a feminine bedroom covered in chintz. Here, smaller plants with rounded shapes or airy, fernlike foliage would fit in better.

Color

When you think about it, color is one of the main reasons for bringing outdoor plants inside. What's sacrificed in terms of longevity is made up for by the almost limitless color of blossoms such plants can provide. Problem is, too many of us who love both color and plants have had the experience of buying a plant only to get it home and discover it clashes with every room of the house. Or we wonder why containers bursting with colorful plants look gorgeous in magazines, but garish when we try it. All that's lacking is some practice and a bit of knowledge about color theory.

Color Theory

Don't let the word theory intimidate you. We're not suggesting that you enroll in art school just to figure out where to place your primroses. In fact, chances are good that you already have an innate sense of the power of various colors. From the time we open that

45

first fragrant box of crayons, most of us have a "favorite" color. And a quick trip through the infant section of a clothing store will prove that we may have come a long way, baby, but color associations still hold strong. Humans will never agree on a universal favorite color (or even whether or not baby boys should wear pink), but we do tend to concur on the effects of various colors. That's all color theory boils down to.

Colors such as yellow, orange, and red are called warm colors. Blue, green, and purple are referred to as cool colors. Cool colors appear to recede from view. Warm colors make objects seem closer. So, in a small room you'd like to feel more spacious, you might place plants with purple or blue flowers in the background. In a location where you'd like plants to really jump out, try red, yellow, or orange flowers.

Of course, whether red flowers would look nice in that room (and the particular shade of red that would work) depends in part on the colors of the walls, furniture, drapes, and carpet in the room. When it comes to combining colors, the simple color wheel shown below is a helpful tool. Colors opposite one another on the wheel are called complementary colors. Placing complementary colors beside each other creates a vibrant, exciting effect. So a windowsill of marigolds in a blue breakfast room might help you wake up and get to work on time. Colors adjacent to one another on the color wheel harmonize and create a calm, relaxing effect. If the blue room you're placing plants in is instead a bedroom, you might want to set a purple viola or a green foliage plant on your bedside table. (Of course, using the term green to refer to plant foliage is a little like using the term flesh-toned to refer to skin color. Plant foliage comes in an amazing array of colors, including silver, purple, red, and chartreuse.)

When filling a container with a group of flowering plants, or placing pots of plants together in a display group, most beginners make the mistake of trying to cram too many colors into one space. A safer bet, which can produce exquisite results, is to instead use plants in varying hues of just one color. Or choose one main color and then add just a bit of the complementary color (or an adjacent color) as an accent. Of course, if you love the effect of six different colors all jumbled together or color combinations that supposedly clash, go with your gut and break the rules. The point of the color wheel and color theory is to help you use plants to decorate your home, not to restrict your creativity.

Texture

Texture, too, comes into play when decorating with plants. The foliage on some plants makes them almost irresistible to touch, while others warn us to keep away. Pay attention to texture when combining plants—are the leaves leathery, fuzzy, hairy, waxy, prickly, bumpy, or smooth? Plants with large, coarse-textured leaves come forward to meet the eye; these plants may be too much for a small room. Those with fine-textured foliage appear to recede from view—handy if you want to make a room appear larger, but keep in mind that these plants could get lost in a large, open room.

Making Up Your Mind

Once you've decided what you want your plants to acheive from a decorating standpoint, you can start to think about choosing specific pants. Look at the photographs in the room-by-room sections of this book, while you sit in the room you're choosing plants for, and see what catches your eye. Keep in mind that, while a room's function will influence your choice of plants, most plants will grow fine anywhere in your home as long as their cultural needs can be met. Books on outdoor gardening and plant encyclopedias can also help you start a plant wish list. Remember, too, that you can always combine outdoor plants with traditional houseplants. While you are thinking about which plants to use, try to visualize the container (or containers) that will achieve the look you're after. The section on containers, which starts on the facing page, will give you plenty of ideas.

Once you have your lists of room conditions, possible plants and container ideas, it's time to go shopping. Don't hesitate to take paint chips, fabric swatches, or wallpaper samples with you to the garden center. If you already have a container you plan to use, take that along, too. All this preparation will be handy if you get to the nursery or garden center and discover that none of the plants you had in mind are available. Or if you have your heart set on red chrysanthemums for your dining room, but can find only yellow ones. Staying flexible will lead you to all sorts of wonderful discoveries you might not make otherwise. Just don't flex so far as to purchase an unhealthy plant. Review the information about buying plants (on page 28) before you head for the stores.

Containers

Finding containers for your plants will be easy. Choosing from the overwhelming selection on the store shelves will be the hard part. At first, you may also find the price tag attached to some of these containers overwhelming, but with careful shopping and a bit of ingenuity, you can own a collection of handsome plant holders without taking out a second mortgage. Mix a couple of the more expensive, beautiful containers you can't resist with a few less-costly but always attractive terra-cotta pots, toss in some baskets (which may already be lurking in your home, just looking for a purpose in life) and a couple of recycled containers (an old cookie tin, a copper pot, or a wooden box), and you're on your way. Decorating with plants is a pleasure when you have a stash of containers ready and waiting. You'll avoid the all-too-common phenomenon of purchasing a plant on impulse only to then let it live out its brief life in its ugly plastic pot while you try to find the right container for it.

Grow Pots and Cachepots

The containers you see in this book are being used as either a grow pot or a cachepot. When you pot a plant directly into a container, the pot is referred to as a grow pot (the pot shown below is an example of this). The plastic nursery pots plants are purchased in can also be called grow pots. When you leave a plant in its purchased pot (or you repot it into a different grow pot) and then place that inside a more decorative container, that decorative container is called a cachepot. (The pot shown above is an example of this.) It's important to remember the difference between the two, not so that you can sound like a gardening snob, but because grow pots and cachepots serve very different purposes. (If you're determined to sound like a gardening snob, pronounce cachepot as *cash-poe;* the more down-to-earth pronunciation sounds like what you win in a poker game.)

A grow pot must have a hole or holes in the bottom for drainage. (You might make an exception for marginal water plants or for plants that won't last longer than a week anyway.) A cachepot doesn't usually have drainage holes; instead, you put gravel or other drainage materials on its

50

bottom and use it as a kind of tall saucer to catch the water that drains out of the grow pot. If you have a container you'd like to use as a cachepot that has a hole in the bottom, simply place a saucer or plastic tray inside the pot before putting down drainage material. You can use a large cachepot to hold an entire arrangement of potted plants. (Place moss strategically to hide the spaces between the pots and the individual pot's rims.) This way, plants with different water and fertilization needs can be grown together in one container. Also, if one plant doesn't do well or stops blooming, you can slip it out and replace it with another without having to repot the entire container.

Types of Containers

Here's a rundown of the most common types of containers.

Terra Cotta

Think of terra-cotta pots as the workhorses of the contained garden; most likely they will make up the bulk of your collection. And for good reason—these clay containers look wonderful with almost every color of flower or foliage and fit in with practically any style of room, while providing the ideal home for almost every kind of plant. Perfect as a grow pot, a terra-cotta pot can also serve as a cachepot.

Terra-cotta pots are porous, so both water and air can pass through their sides. This helps prevent overwatered plants from drowning. On the other hand, it also means that plants in these pots must be watered more often than those in nonporous containers. (Soak a clay pot in water before using it to repot a plant; otherwise, the pot will suck the water right out of the new plant's soil.)

Terra-cotta pots (especially the larger ones) tend to be heavy. This keeps them from toppling over easily (a problem with lightweight pots), but it also makes them a pain in the back to move once you've filled them with soil and plants.

Plastic

Plastic containers are lightweight, inexpensive, and durable. Because they aren't porous like terra cotta, plastic pots hold moisture longer, so their occupants require less frequent waterings. Of course, this carries with it the danger that plants in plastic will be overwatered and drown. If you're willing to pay more, you can find plastic that looks very much like terra cotta. But let's face it, the majority of plastic pots look plastic and just plain ugly. These pots are best used as the undergarments of the container world—as grow pots discreetly hidden beneath more attractive attire.

Ceramic

The biggest problem with ceramic containers is that there are so many colorful and delightfully patterned ones available, it's hard to resist the temptation to buy every last one that catches your eye. Doing so will hurt more than just your budget. Unless you're an absolute genius at mixing colors and patterns, all those decorative ceramic containers are likely to compete with each other and with the plants inside. Of course, you can find ceramic containers in solid, subdued colors, and one or two boldly decorated pots will look stunning in the right setting. Just make sure they'll work with the decor of the room you'll be placing them in. Ceramic pots with very busy patterns tend to look best with foliage plants rather than flowering plants inside.

Many ceramic pots come with drainage holes and even saucers; these can be used as grow pots. Those without drain holes must be used as cachepots (unless you have a plant that likes wet feet).

Concrete

Concrete containers, because of their bulk and weight, are usually used outdoors, but they can work well indoors as long as you take care to place them where they won't damage furniture or carpets. Containers made from concrete can vary in appearance from rustic imitation-stone troughs to elegant urns. Just remember that a large concrete planter filled with soil and plants will be heavy—you might need to place your concrete container in its permanent location first, and then fill it with soil and plants.

Baskets

Baskets, with their natural materials and wonderful woven textures, make perfect containers for all sorts of indoor gardens. You can pur-

term plants. Just remember that metal containers set in full sun can heat up very quickly and "cook" plant roots, and some metals must be treated so they don't leach metallic elements or rust into the soil. Keep in mind, too, that long-term plants will eventually need repotting. If your metal container is heavy, you'll be glad you used it as a cachepot rather than a grow pot when repotting time comes around.

chase baskets that come with waterproof liners at a gardening center, but these tend to be mass-produced and not nearly as attractive as the baskets you may already have about your house. Either line such a basket with plastic and then fill it with soil, or—to make it easier on both yourself and the basket—simply place a saucer or a liner in its bottom and then use the basket as a cachepot.

Cane, willow, twigs, vines, pine needles, grass, and palm leaves are just some of the materials used to weave baskets. Consider both the material and style of the basket when deciding if it will fit with your decor and the plant (or plants) that will go inside. A rustic twig basket of spring bulbs would look fetching in a cottage-style room, while a basket woven from palm leaves containing a tropical plant would be right at home in most beach houses or sunrooms.

Metal

Metal containers can be as funky as an old chipped enamel bucket or as elegant as an antique bronze urn. Decorative food tins, which might not be appropriate for houseplants, can make charming containers for short-

Recycled Containers

Take a trip up into your attic, out to your garage, or through a flea market, and you'll discover all sorts of objects just waiting to be turned into plant containers. Plumbing fixtures, cast-off kitchenware, old crates, and even toys can

What Lies Beneath

Potted plants, like babies, leak regularly. They're supposed to. Think of saucers as the diapers of the plant world, something you can't do without. If you try, one of two things will happen: you'll ruin your furniture and carpet, or you'll underwater your plants. And just as babies become unhappy if they sit around in a wet diaper too long, plants too will sulk if you leave them sitting in a wet saucer. (Always check the saucer half an hour after watering and empty any standing water.)

Plastic and terra-cotta saucers are widely available, but plates and bowls with decorative rims can serve as saucy substitutes. Unglazed terra-cotta saucers allow moisture to seep through and ruin furniture and floors; set them on protective mats or slip clear plastic saucers inside or under them. Whatever you use for a

become homes for plants if you keep the following points in mind.

Grow pot or cachepot? If it's going to be a grow pot, it needs to have a hole (or holes) for drainage. If it doesn't, will you be able to drill through the material? An item that will be used as a cachepot must be waterproof or able to hold a waterproof saucer in its bottom.

Shape. Commercial pots are wider at the top than at the bottom because this shape makes it easiest to eventually remove the plant and soil. If

you choose a container with a narrow opening at the top, you'll have a tougher job when it comes time to repot; in fact, in some cases you may have to break the container to get the plant out with its root system intact. Containers with this shape can also be difficult to water and may not be able to provide the plant's roots with a sufficient amount of air.

Weight. When your container-to-be is filled with soil, plant, and then water, will you be able to move it? If not, you'd better plan to use it as a cachepot and make sure it looks good on the floor.

saucer, it should be at least as wide as the top rim of the grow pot it sits under, preferably a bit wider. When you place a grow pot in a cachepot, you can use the cachepot as a kind of saucer (usually with gravel in its bottom for drainage), or you can place a saucer inside the cachepot (under the grow pot) to collect runoff. (If you have more than one grow pot in a cachepot, you can place a large plastic saucer inside the cachepot, instead of giving each pot its own saucer.)

Matching Plants to Pot

Matching plants and containers is one of those skills that will become almost instinctual once you've had a little practice. Whether you start with the plant (or group of plants) and look for a container or have a container you love in need of a plant, keep a few key things in mind.

Size and proper drainage are the most important factors. The pot should be able to accommodate the plant's root ball with about 1 inch (2.5 cm) of space on the sides and up to 6 inches (15.2 cm) of space at the bottom. This space, obviously, will soon be replaced with soil. The typical beginning container gardener chooses too large a container for the plant. When this happens, the soil stays wet and the plant's roots rot. Of course, with short-term outdoorplants you can be less particular about giving the roots the right size home, but you do want a pleasing balance between the container and the part of the plant that shows. A safe rule of thumb is for the plant to be one and a half times the width or height of its container.

The style of your container, the plant, and the room they'll inhabit also come into play. Tulips can be elegant in a crystal vase, sporty in a simple clay pot, or playful in an old washtub. But not every plant will work in every container.

A fine-leaved plant might be overwhelmed by a solid cement container, while a large-leafed plant may appear too robust for a delicate-looking bowl.

When it comes to color, you can go in one of two directions. Play it safe and stay with containers in muted colors or terra cotta, or go wild and be prepared to make some mistakes on the way to discovering dazzling combinations. Use the color wheel on page 47 and the information about color theory on page 45 to help you choose containers in colors that will bring out the best in both their plants and the room in which they're placed. If you want to play it safe, remember that terra cotta looks terrific with just about every color plant and goes with practically any style of decor.

etting plants, containers, and rooms to work together is like so many other things in life: sometimes it takes careful forethought and planning, and sometimes it all falls together serendipitously. The room-by-room selection of plantings that follows offers information, instructions, and inspiration. Use it as a tool to carefully reproduce what you see or as fuel to fire up your own creativity. The room divisions are meant to guide but by no means restrict you. While the function of a room will influence your plant and container choice, most plants will be happy in any room as long as their growing needs can be met. (In fact, wise indoor gardeners know that moving plants about from room to room is often the best way to meet their light, temperature, and humidity needs.) At the same time, it does pay to think about the functions of your rooms. Which are hubs of busy activity, which are retreats where you relax and unwind, and which are areas where you entertain? Will plants be subjected to grease or hair spray; will containers be at the mercy of frantic cooks or rambunctious pets or children? Take your own home, taste, and lifestyle into account as you sample the offerings that follow. Then break out the potting soil; it's time to start bringing the outdoors in.

Room-by-room
gardens

Coleus Combination

After falling out

of fashion for a while, coleus are hot again, putting on their spectacular display in shade gardens everywhere. A cinch to grow, coleus can be equally impressive indoors. This large planting in a single container makes the perfect companion for the red woodstove, while its foliage gives a playful nod to the leaf pattern on the nearby chair. The plant's recent surge in popularity has led to the development of over 200 varieties, with amind-boggling array of leaf forms and colors.

Indoors, coleus like well-drained soil, so pot your plants directly into a container with good drainage, and place the container in bright, but not direct, light. Keep the soil evenly moist (in summer, you may need to water every day), and feed the plants with an all-purpose water-soluble fertilizer every few weeks. Your coleus will do well in average indoor temperatures and will appreciate frequent misting to help increase the humidity. To keep this rapid grower tidy, you'll probably have to prune it from time to time. Just use a pair of sharp scissors to snip stems right above the spot where a leaf sprouts. Two new stems will grow at each cut, so the more you prune, the bushier the plant will become. Because of this, coleus is easy to train into a ball-shaped topiary standard (see page 65 for instructions).

Garden Miscellany

Growing coleus from cuttings is easy. Just cut about a 4-inch-long (10.2 cm) piece from the tip of a stem, and stick it in a small pot of potting soil. (Use rooting hormone powder if you have some, but coleus roots so readily that it's usually not necessary.) Place the pot in bright, but not direct, light. Keep the soil moist until small roots form. Pinch back the tip of the plant to encourage side branches. You may also have luck propagating coleus by simply sticking a small cutting in a glass of water.

Turn a living room

into a late-winter/early-spring garden nook with flowering plants that are potted in painted French flower buckets. Available at florists and gift shops, these pails from French flower markets make colorful blooms look right at home.

Because these buckets have no drainage holes, your best bet will be to keep the hydrangea and white cape primrose in their plastic grow pots and use the buckets as cachepots; then you can simply lift the the plants out and carry them to the sink for watering. Since calla lilies are one of the few houseplants that need soggy soil, they can be planted directly into the flower bucket. Hydrangeas will do best in bright light and perhaps some direct sun from an eastern window. They need cool temperatures and continually moist, but not soggy, soil. Be careful if you plant directly into the flower bucket—you don't want hydrangeas to sit in water. The calla lilies can be placed in a southern window but they'll need the protection that shutters, blinds, or a sheer curtain can provide from the noon sun on warm days. Since callas thrive in wet soil, be sure to water frequently. The cape primrose (which should be potted in a shallow grow pot) needs bright, but not direct, light. It likes temperatures a little warmer than that preferred by the other two plants, so keep it away from cool windows. Its soil should be kept evenly moist. All of these plants will appreciate having their leaves misted (just be careful not to wet the cape primrose leaves too much).

Garden Miscellany

If you live in a climate where temperatures stay above -5°F (-21°C), you can plant your hydrangea outside in the spring in a sunny to partly shady spot. (In colder areas you can grow the hydrangea outdoors in its container for the summer.) After flowering, cut stems back to half their height. Fertilize the plant throughout the growing season with a balanced water-soluble fertilizer.

Leatherleaf Sedge

Sometimes simple is best, as the striking silhouettes of these leatherleaf sedges in rusty metal containers illustrate. This ornamental plant is valued in the garden for its copper-colored foliage with curly tips (it's sometimes referred to as "curly sedge"). Indoors, its unique color and form will complement a variety of decors.

The bronze blades of leatherleaf sedge look particularly striking in copper-colored or rusted metal containers. If you use pots without drainage holes, such as the ones in the photo, place a layer of gravel in the bottom for drainage or use the containers as cachepots. The plants will do best in a location where they receive bright sun, but they can take center stage for a short spell on a coffee table in the middle of a room. Keep the soil continually moist, but not soggy. After a few weeks indoors, the sedge will need to be grown outdoors as a container plant on a patio or in the garden.

Garden Miscellany

The botanical name for leatherleaf sedge is Carex buchananii. *The name* Carex *comes from the Greek word* kerio, *meaning "to cut." It refers to the tiny saw-tooth edges found on the foliage of sedges.*

Topiary, one of the

oldest forms of garden art, takes on a modern look with this myrtle standard and its winsome skirt of carex grass. Because myrtle responds well to frequent pruning, it's one of the easiest plants to train into the ball and stick shape of a standard. (Topiary has become so popular that gardeners in a hurry should be able to find myrtle already shaped into a standard.) The carex grass (available at nurseries and garden centers) is planted right into the same container, on either side of the myrtle.

Potted in well-drained soil that's kept continually moist and is lightly fertilized, this combination should work well indoors or out from May through September in bright, indirect light. After that you'll want to plant the carex grass outdoors for the winter, but the myrtle topiary can be wintered over indoors. To train myrtle into a standard, start with a young plant with a straight center stem, remove two thirds of the bottom branches, and attach the stem loosely to a bamboo stake. Clip the tips of the sideshoots on the top third of the plant so they bush out. As the plant develops more leaves, continue to clip into the desired ball shape.

Garden Miscellany

Myrtle bears white flowers in summer and blue or purple berries in the fall. Its shiny, aromatic leaves are used in potpourri. Myrtle is considered the herb of fertility and love. A Ukrainian custom calls for the mother of the bride to weave sprigs of myrtle into a wreath the bride wears under her veil.

Miniature Cattail

Who'd have guessed

that this humble swamp plant could look so swank in the right setting? The slender, upright reeds of a miniature cattail look positively urbane in this handsome container topped with moss. The plant's tall, dramatic profile is just right for the high-ceilinged living room of this contemporary loft. An additional decorative touch will come when the cattail's characteristic brown flower spikes appear.

The popularity of small backyard ponds has made marginal plants such as this relatively inexpensive and easy to find. To grow indoors in a container, it will need wet soil and bright, direct sun. Once you've potted your cattail, moss can be added around the base of the reeds for decorative effect. Feed the plant by inserting food tabs for aquatic plants into the soil (follow manufacturer's directions) or simply water with a weak dose of liquid fertilizer every couple of weeks. If your cattail starts to languish indoors, you can move it outside to the patio or add it to a water garden. Take care though, cattails can be invasive if planted directly into the soil or added to earth-bottom ponds.

Garden Miscellany

Native Americans used cattails for food and medicine. They also wove the plant's reeds into mats (sometimes used to cover wigwams), baskets, and even toys.

Inexpensive, easy-to-find

annual bedding plants can pack a visual wallop when you choose complementary colors and plant them in a playful strawberry pot. The added height from the wood pedestal turns these marigolds and ageratums into a fountain of flowers that adds to the contemporary color scheme while enlivening this sparsely furnished section of a room.

To plant the strawberry pot, first fill it with potting soil up to the first set of pockets. Plant one ageratum seedling in each pocket with the rootball extending in toward the center of the container. Plant each pocket on this level, and then add soil up to the next set of pockets. Use the same method to plant these pockets with ageratums. Continue planting the ageratums in this manner until the soil is about ½ inch (1.3 cm) below the top rim of the pot. Then plant the marigolds in the top of the pot. Marigold flowers will rot if they get too much water, so stick the watering can's spout under their foliage and water slowly. You may need to water each individual pocket, also. Place the container where the plants will receive lots of light, but protection from direct midday sun. Keep the soil evenly moist, and pinch or shear spent flowers to keep the planting blooming all summer.

Mandevilla Vine

Do you find yourself

rushing around all the time? Maybe you need a mandevilla in your corner. Tall or climbing plants are often just what's needed to fill an unused corner of a room. As this vine twines its way up a trellis, it seems to say, "What's your hurry? Pour yourself a tall, cool drink and sit for a spell." It will be hard not to stop and admire the plant's large pink, white, yellow, or red funnel-shaped flowers and dark, glossy leaves. The flowers, which darken as they age, usually have yellow or orange-tinged throats and are fragrant in some varieties.

Pot your mandevilla directly into a container with well-drained soil. If the plant you purchase is large enough, it may be sold with its own short trellis. Otherwise, take care when adding a trellis to the container not to injure any part of the plant. Place the plant where it will receive bright light: (near a southern or western window, it will need some protection from the sun in summer). During the growing season, mandevilla should be watered when the soil surface feels dry (water slowly, so you're sure to drench the soil) and may be fed every other month with an all-purpose water-soluble fertilizer. If your mandevilla seems unhappy indoors, you can let it summer outside in a partly shaded location with protection from direct afternoon sun. This plant won't tolerate temperatures below 40°F (4°C) though, so in most climates, you'll need to move it back inside in the fall. Water sparingly, and don't fertilize the vine while it rests during the late fall and winter. If you prune heavily in late winter or early spring, the plant will bloom better.

Garden Miscellany

The mandevilla vine is a native of Central and South America. It was named for Henry Mandeville (1773-1861), the British ambassador to Argentina who introduced the plant to English gardeners.

Lily, Ivy & Bird's Nest Fern

Take indoor gardening to

new heights with this elegant combination of lily, ivy, and bird's nest fern framed by pussy willow branches. A small detail such as the ivy trailing over the basket's edge can help an arrangement blend in with its setting. The tall pussy willow branches, on the other hand, give the planting the stature to keep it from hiding in the corner. Lilies can be found in a range of colors, so adapting this garden to coordinate with your living room decor will be a breeze.

Lilies will only last a matter of weeks indoors, but the other plants will grow inside indefinitely, so keep each plant in its own grow pot, and use the basket as a cachepot. Be sure to remove any decorative foil from the lily pot, so it can drain properly. When the lily fades, you can pull it out, pot and all, and replace it with another potted plant. All of these plants will do best in bright indirect light, continually moist soil, and cool (but not cold) temperatures. (The ivy should be watered sparingly in winter but never allowed to dry out

completely.) Mist the foliage to help increase the humidity around this planting.

Instructions for forcing pussy willows can be found on page 99. To make the trellis of pussy willows, simply tie the branches together with twine or raffia. Bits of moss can be hot-glued to the joints for a decorative touch.

Garden Miscellany

Instructions for forcing pussy willows can be found on page 99.

To keep lilies attractive as long as possible, purchase a plant with only one or two partly open flowers and three or four unopened buds. Once the flowers mature, remove the yellow anthers before the pollen sheds. Deadhead flowers when they wither. You can plant lilies out in the garden once all danger of frost has passed; they'll need one year of rest before they begin to bloom again, usually in June or July.

Caladiums & New Guinea Impatiens

Got guests coming

for dinner tonight? Take three inexpensive potted plants, a container, and some moss, and transform them into a lovely centerpiece in about the amount of time it takes to set the table! The patterned foliage of the caladiums would be too much combined with most flowers, but it looks just right with these white New Guinea impatiens. The plants are low enough to permit conversation across the table and have no strong fragrance to compete with the food.

To save on both mess and time, use a waterproof container as a cachepot—simply place the potted plants in it, and then cover up the pots and any space left with moss. A few hours as a centerpiece will do these plants no harm, but find a more permanent location for them with bright, indirect light, warm temperatures, and fairly high humidity. (You can increase their humidity by misting the leaves occasionally, but avoid getting the blossoms of the impatiens wet.)

The soil for both impatiens and caladiums should be kept consistently moist, but not soggy. In summer, the impatiens may need to be watered every day. The caladiums will last through the summer before their leaves begin to wither in preparation for dormancy. You can toss them into the compost pile at that point or gradually withhold water until the foliage shrivels completely. Then allow the soil to dry out thoroughly before removing the tubers from the pot and pulling away the dead leaves. The tubers can then be stored in dry peat moss, perlite, or vermiculite until the following spring. You may be able to keep the impatiens going indoors through the winter, but they probably won't flower much.

Garden Miscellany

Impatiens get their name from the seed capsules' habit of popping open and shooting out seeds at the slightest touch. They are also sometimes called "touch-me-nots" for this reason. In Great Britain, impatiens are nicknamed "busy Lizzies," but in the United States, their nickname is "patient Lucy."

Autumn Asters

Autumn comes, and the garden begins to slow down, to prepare for its wintry sleep. A pot of cheery asters in a window will make those golden days seem to linger a little longer. Placing this handsome pot filled with tall blooms by the window draws much-deserved attention to this sunlit nook.

Most asters bloom in late summer to autumn, so the plants can usually still be found in nurseries and garden centers then. Asters already growing outdoors benefit from division every few years; if you're bringing a plant in from the garden, follow the instructions on page 29. Inside, asters (which will survive only as temporary guests) need as much light as possible and continually moist soil. You can pot an aster directly into a grow pot or leave a purchased plant in its plastic container and slip it into a decorative cachepot, as shown in the photo, but remember in either case that good drainage is necessary for these plants to stay healthy. Since asters tend to be prone to diseases, you'll also want to provide adequate air circulation.

Garden Miscellany

John Parkinson, herbalist to King Charles, prescribed aster for "the biting of a mad dogge, the greene herbe being beaten with old hogs grease, and applyed."

Ferns, Impatiens & Vinca

If you have a decorative

container you'd like to show off but don't want to overwhelm with a complicated mix of plants, try this elegant trio. Japanese painted fern, dwarf white impatiens, and variegated vinca make a lovely combination that enhances rather than detracts from the beauty of this unique container. Here the plants and the stoneware pot complement the white hues that surround them.

All of these plants can be potted directly into a container with good drainage, or you can keep the plants in their individual pots and use a decorative container as a cachepot. These plants need bright, indirect light and consistently moist soil. After a couple of months indoors, move the container to a lightly shaded spot on a patio or porch. You may be able to overwinter the impatiens and vinca (also known as periwinkle) indoors, but the Japanese painted fern is a hardy perennial that needs to be planted outside for the winter.

Garden Miscellany

Both white blossoms and variegated foliage look lovely by candlelight. Plants with silver or gray foliage also look fetching in the soft glow of a candle. If you're choosing plants to create a centerpiece for the dining table, remember that white flowers are often fragrant, and their heavy scent can interfere with the enjoyment of the meal.

Chrysanthemums

Bring a bright touch of

autumn to the table with cheerful chrysanthemums. Purchased inexpensively at a gardening center and then popped into square glass vases filled first with sand and then potting soil, these maroon mums are the perfect complement to this dining room's gold walls and vintage tableware. (Place a piece of coffee filter between the sand and the soil to keep the sand cleaner.) Finding mums that work with your decor should be easy—nurseries have figured out how to have pot chrysanthemums bloom in just about every color at any time of year.

Although these plants will be fine for at least a long weekend in their festive sand and soil homes, in more favorable conditions chrysanthemums can be kept for six to eight weeks indoors. They like bright light, but midday sun can burn the flowers, so an east- or west-facing window would be best. Keep the soil continually moist; and mist the leaves occasionally. The plants will last longest if kept in cool temperatures (in the 60 to 65°F [15 to 18°C] range is ideal). Once pot chrysanthemums have stopped blooming, you can try replanting them into your garden.

Garden Miscellany

Chrysanthemums have symbolized the scholar in retirement since the 4th century, when the Chinese poet Tao Yuan Ming refused a high government post because he said he preferred to pick chrysanthemums, entertain his friends, and get drunk. His chrysanthemum gardens were so revered that after his death, his town was renamed the City of Chrysanthemums.

Begonia Basket

A copper basket full

of begonias can add just the right touch to your dining room decor, and you can put it together in a spare half hour one afternoon. With the current number of begonia hybrids estimated at more than 1,000, finding one in a color that works with your decor should be easy. Situated near this opulent oil painting, the plant in its ample pot completes the still-life effect.

Use your container as a cachepot, and simply set as many plants as needed (grow pot and all) inside. Begonias don't like wet leaves, so they should be removed from the container and watered carefully at the sink (you can also use the bottom-watering method described on page 17). Once in the container, the grow pots will be hidden by the plants' large leaves, so you probably won't even need any moss to hide them. Begonias need bright light away from direct sunlight and evenly moist soil. Remove spent blooms regularly, and water sparingly once the plants have stopped blooming. In hot dry weather, mist the air around the begonias to improve the humidity, but because these plants are susceptible to powdery mildew, don't wet the leaves.

Garden Miscellany

Here are some troubleshooting tips for begonias:
Yellow leaves:
Try providing more water or moving into brighter light.
Flower buds drop:
Improve humidity or give more water.
Brown tips on leaves:
Improve humidity.
Stems are thin and leggy:
Move to brighter light.

Taro, Sweet Potato Vine, Mother Fern & Ivy

Who says foliage plants

are boring? The huge, deep purple leaves of taro 'Jet Black Wonder' and the meandering sweet potato vine 'Blackie' look terrific with the vibrant green of a mother fern and the variegated foliage of an English ivy. Arranged in a rusty urn placed on the floor, the planting draws your eye to the attractive wall clock above it. If you yearn for an urn, but cast iron is too costly for your budget (or too heavy for your back), investigate the attractive, affordable, and lightweight polyethylene and fiberglass urns now available.

Pot these plants directly into urns with drainage holes (you'll have to use a saucer to protect your floor from water runoff). If your urn doesn't drain, then use it as a cachepot: pot the plants into a separate container and place it on a layer of gravel or pebbles inside the urn. These plants will do best in bright, filtered light, in an area with high humidity and warm temperatures. Keep the soil consistently moist. If you have a hard time finding taro (*Colocasia*), you could substitute the similar-looking and more widely available elephant ears (*Alocasia*). This container of plants could live indoors year-round as long as its cultural needs are met.

Garden Miscellany

In theory, the tubers of both sweet potato vine and taro are edible, but to be safe, enjoy them as ornamental plants only. Taro must be cooked properly or it can burn your skin and mucous membranes badly, and ornamental plants purchased commercially have often been exposed to toxic chemicals.

Canna Lily

When you start to feel

a bit bored with your decor, go wild with an exotic canna lily. It's one of the few plants that's loved for both its flowers and its foliage. In many climates, outdoor cannas have to be dug up before winter, so why not place one in a pot and let it light up your indoors for a spell? The multicolored, striped leaves of this canna look terrific with the deep gold walls of this dining room.

If you purchase a canna instead of taking one from the garden, you can simply stick it, grow pot and all, into a decorative cachepot. Otherwise, plant your canna into a pot that's 16 to 20 inches (40.6 to 50.8 cm) in diameter. Place the plant in a well-lit site where it will receive at least four hours of direct sun each day. Make sure it's in a location that doesn't get too cold at night, as cannas are tropical plants that cannot tolerate temperatures much below 58°F (14°C). Water regularly to provide the plant with evenly moist soil; if the soil dries out too much, the leaf color will fade. When growth becomes lackluster, you can cut the entire plant back to force new growth. If you can meet its sunlight needs, you may be able to keep your canna growing indoors all winter. You can then reward the plant with a summer vacation outdoors (just don't move it straight into hot, direct sunlight, or you'll burn the leaves).

Garden Miscellany

Because the seeds of canna look like shotgun pellets, the plant earned the nickname "Indian shot." Native South Americans strung the hard, round seeds to make necklaces and other jewelry. In the 16th century, Spanish explorers brought the seeds back to Spain where they were turned into rosary beads.

Daffodils, Tulips, Chrysanthemums, African Violets & Ivy

What house guest

wouldn't feel welcome in a bedroom abloom with this spring basket? Because the basket serves as a cache-pot for the individually potted plants, you can put this cheerful garden together quickly with little mess. Just place a waterproof saucer in the basket's bottom, and then arrange the potted plants. Tuck the ivy in last, twining a bit of the vine up your basket's handle, and then cover the spaces between the pots with moss. (If you follow the instructions for forcing bulbs found on page 31, you can create a spring basket in midwinter; forced bulbs can also be bought potted and ready to bloom, starting in mid to late winter.)

This combination will do well in bright light; it won't tolerate direct sun. Let the soil surface of each pot dry out slightly between waterings, and mist occasionally to increase the humidity. These flowers will last longest if you keep them away from heat sources and provide cool evening temperatures. The exception to this is the African violet, which doesn't like temperatures much below 60°F (15°C). Place it in the front of the basket, so you can remove it easily if the temperature in the room will get too chilly overnight. (It can survive temperatures down to 50°F [10°C] if its soil is fairly dry.) You may also want to water the African violet when it's out of the basket, since it looks best if you avoid spilling water on its leaves.

Garden Miscellany

Add some colored eggs, and you could turn this arrangement into a fetching Easter basket. Or you can make a smaller version of this basket and hang it from a friend's or neighbor's doorknob for May Day. Tradition calls for you to ring the bell and then run quickly out of sight.

Passionflower Vine

Want to add a little

passion to your bedroom? Let this gorgeous flowering vine lend a touch of the tropics to the decor. This robust climber can reach up to 20 feet (6.2 m) in height, sends out large, breathtakingly beautiful blooms all summer long, and even produces edible fruit. The plant has been strategically placed here to take advantage of the light without obscuring the attractive view out the bedroom windows.

Passionflowers can be grown indoors indefinitely, so pot yours in a large container with good, well-drained soil. The exotic appearance of this plant may mislead you into thinking it's finicky, but it's actually quite easy to grow indoors in a container. You will, however, need a location where it can receive at least four hours of direct sun each day (you may want to let your vine summer outside, where it can receive both sun and pollination). Passionflowers need moist soil while actively growing; this may mean daily watering in summer. Reduce waterings slightly in fall and winter, when the plant is dormant. The passion vine also needs a fairly warm, humid environment, and it will appreciate an occasional misting. This plant needs to be fertilized twice a month during the growing season with an all-purpose fertilizer. Prune your vine to within 6 inches (15.2 cm) of the soil or to six to eight buds in early spring to encourage flowering. If you keep your passionflower slightly pot-bound, it will produce more of the exotic blossoms.

Garden Miscellany

You'll have to hand-pollinate your vine if you want it to produce passion fruit indoors. To do so, use a small artist's paintbrush to transfer pollen from the yellow downward-facing anthers to the tips of the stigmas (these are at the ends of the three-part structure in the center of each blossom). Flowers that have been successfully pollinated will remain attached to the vine after they've closed. The fruits are ripe when they fall from the vine.

It doesn't matter how

many dreary winters we've been through; the small miracle of spring always catches us slightly by surprise. You can capture the heady scents and sensational blossoms of spring in a single basket—while the snow is still piling up outside, if you follow the instructions on page 31 for forcing bulbs. The busy toile de Jouy wallpaper and fabric combined with the full, colorful blooms create a comforting, opulent mood in this bedroom.

Because different types of bulbs require different lengths of time chilling before they can be coaxed into flowering, combinations such as this, with tulips, daffodils, and muscari (also know as grape hyacinth), work best when individual pots of bulbs are grouped together in a cachepot. In this case, we've used a twig basket with a plastic saucer in its bottom, and covered the pot rims with moss and fresh green clumps of grass. (To grow grass indoors, simply sow seed in a shallow pan filled with potting soil.) If you haven't forced bulbs, you can usually find them for sale,

ready to bloom, starting in mid-January. Although bulbs need good light while the leaves are greening and the buds are setting, after that, you can place them wherever they look best in your home, as long as the spot is cool and out of direct sunlight. Let the soil surface of each pot dry out slightly between waterings (you may find it easiest to remove the pots from the basket and water them in the sink; then return them after they've had their drinks, and rearrange the moss). The flowers will last longer if you keep them away from heat sources and as cool as possible (without freezing) in the evening. See the instructions on page 33 if you'd like to try to plant forced bulbs back out in the garden when they're done blooming.

Garden Miscellany

During Holland's Tulipomania of the 1630s, single tulip bulbs sometimes sold for over 3,000 guilders. A pamphlet written at the time pointed out that such a large amount of money could have purchased the following goods: 8 fat pigs, 4 fat oxen, 12 fat sheep, 24 tons of wheat, 48 tons of rye, 2 hogsheads of wine, 4 barrels of beer, 2 tons of butter, 1,000 pounds of cheese, a silver drinking cup, a pack of clothes, a bed with mattress and bedding, and a boat!

Miniature Roses

A bouquet of cut roses

is both costly and short-lived, but this silver vase planted with miniature roses will provide affordable romance that can later be transplanted into the garden. More than 200 types of these dainty roses are available; they come in every color but blue and are easily found in garden centers, nurseries, and groceries stores from midwinter through summer. Try combining two colors for a unique look—a bit of Spanish moss draped at the vase's edge can add a dramatic touch. In this room, where rich color sets the mood, the roses, though dainty in scale, play beautifully off the deep rose walls.

Depending on the drainage of your container, you can either pot miniature roses directly into the container, or you can keep the roses in a grow pot and use a decorative container as a cachepot. (Place plenty of gravel or pebbles for drainage in the bottom of a vase-shaped container.) Locate your plants where they'll receive bright light all day long and several hours of direct sun, but make sure they're not placed near a window that's drafty. Keep their soil evenly moist while they're actively growing; once they've finished blooming, allow the soil to dry out slightly between waterings. Roses like high humidity, but they also require good air-circulation. You can set the container on a pebble tray (see page 21 for instructions) or mist the leaves early in the day, but make sure the leaves don't stay wet overnight. Feed your roses every two weeks in spring and summer with a balanced water-soluble fertilizer. During the fall and winter, feed once a month with a half-strength solution.

Garden Miscellany

After miniature roses have finished blooming, they need to rest for several months before blooming again. During this time, keep them as cool as possible, but don't let them freeze. They may need to be pruned after dormancy to encourage compact growth. You can transplant your roses into the garden once the threat of frost is past. Keep them well watered and fed during the growing season, and prune them back 3 to 4 inches (7.6 to 10.2 cm) in the spring.

Perennial Bowl

This combination of perennials would be a striking, yet low-maintenance, summer guest in your home. A study in form and texture, this indoor garden contains the broad leaves of hostas (one variegated), Lily of the Nile with its straplike leaves and exploding firecracker of dark blue flowers, the scalloped burgundy foliage and airy spires of coral bells, the brilliant blue flowers of plumbago, and the golden yellow leaves of creeping Jenny. Its significant mass holds up well beside the large armoire, which could dwarf a smaller planting.

If you use a large, heavy container like this stone bowl, place the empty container in the desired location first, and then add the soil and plants. If your planter doesn't provide drainage, you'll need to add a layer of gravel on the bottom and use the container as a cachepot. This group of plants needs bright indirect light.

Water thoroughly, and allow the soil surface to dry out a bit between waterings. Fertilize at planting time with a time-release fertilizer. This combination should last indoors for a couple of months; it will probably last longest if the plants are potted directly into a container that provides good drainage.

Garden Miscellany

This container garden can be moved outdoors, but the Lily of the Nile must be wintered indoors in cold climates. Think twice before letting creeping Jenny out of its container. It's a rampant grower that may creep into your lawn and become a pest.

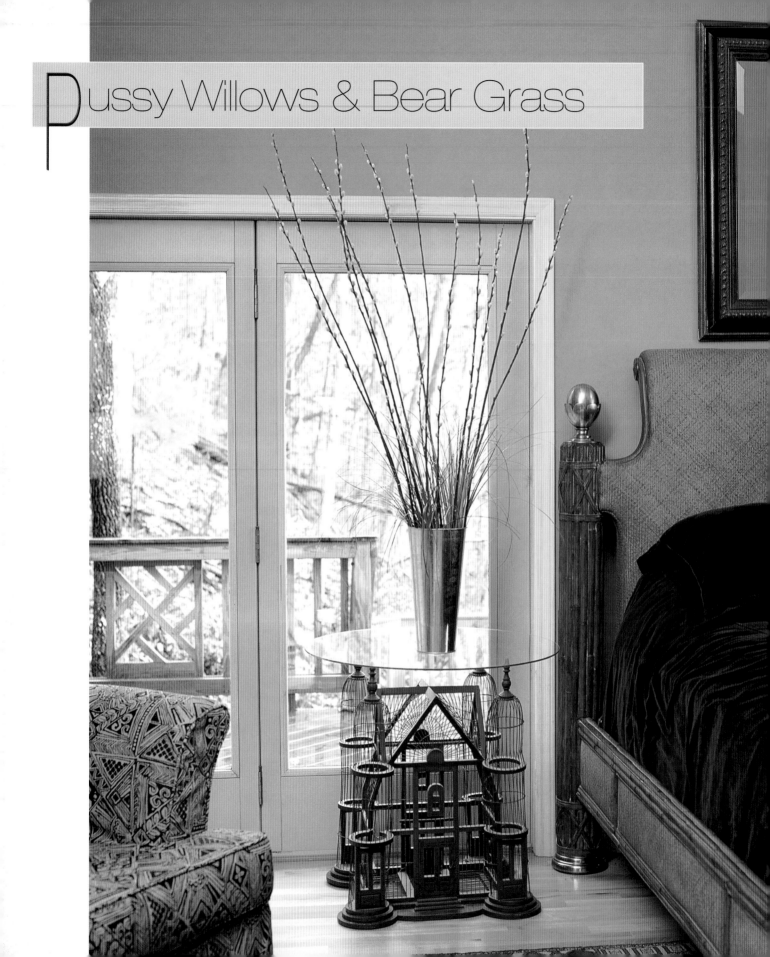

Pussy Willows & Bear Grass

This striking duet

of pussy willows and bear grass brings simple beauty to life. Finding a plant to match the scale of the furniture in this room is a tall order to fill, but these 5-foot-tall (1.5 m) forced pussy willows branches are up to the task. Bear grass (actually the foliage of a plant in the lily family) is available from florist shops. Pussy willows can be cut from outside or purchased from florists in the spring, or forced indoors in mid-winter.

Forcing branches into early bloom is much simpler than forcing bulbs. It consists of little more than cutting branches and sticking them in warm water indoors. Just cut the branches after they've had at least six weeks of cold weather (this will be around the end of January in most climates), preferably on a warmer than usual day. If you soak them in a tub in tepid water for a few hours, the bud scales will loosen faster. After their soak, cut at least 1 inch (2.5 cm) from each stem; then place the stems in a container filled with tepid water. Very tall branches will tip over easily, so use a substantial container; if the arrangement still feels top-heavy, add sand or pebbles to the bottom (this can also help with positioning the branches). The bear grass can also be stuck right into the container of water; it stays attractive for weeks. The soft, silvery pussy willows should emerge in a couple of weeks; the closer it is to their natural bloom time, the sooner they'll open. If you remove them from the water once they open, they'll dry nicely and keep for years.

Garden Miscellany

Use this same method to coax the branches of all sorts of shrubs to bloom indoors in late winter. Once you experience seemingly lifeless sticks unfurling their delicate blossoms and tender new leaves, you'll want to "branch out" and experiment. Some favorites for forcing include forsythia, quince, redbud, cherry, witch hazel, maple, lilac, and spirea (bridal wreath).

Woodland Planter

This group of elegant

plants might seem a strange choice for a rustic bark container, but it works splendidly, perhaps in part because this orchid actually grows on tree trunks in its natural habitat. The marriage of sophistication and rusticity also matches the tone of the eclectic decor surrounding this bedroom writing table.

The butterfly or moth orchid (*Phalaenopsis*) can bloom for months and is one of the easiest orchids to grow. It does, however, need to be planted in a special orchid mix instead of potting soil, so keep each plant in this group in a grow pot and use the main container as a cachepot. Set the cachepot near an east-facing window, situated so the jasmine will get some direct sun and the rest of the plants will receive bright light. The cape primrose needs to be potted in a shallow pot and placed farthest from a cool window. Keep its soil moist, and feed it with 10-10-10 fertilizer every month while blooming. Feed the orchid with 10-20-10 orchid fertilizer every three months and keep its soil moist but not soggy. The Chinese painted fern (*Pteris tremula*) needs evenly moist soil all year, and should be fed with a 10-10-10 fertilizer every other month. Keep the jasmine's soil very moist and feed it monthly with a 20-10-10 fertilizer. Mist this group's foliage to increase the humidity, but be careful not to wet the cape primrose leaves too much.

Garden Miscellany

You may be able to get your butterfly orchid to flower almost year-round if you prune the flower stalk to just below the lowest bloom after the flowers have faded. A couple of weeks of cooler temperatures (but not below 55°F [13°C]) in the fall should also increase flowering.

Sedum & Sempervivum

It's amazing how

the right plants and the perfect setting can make something old look positively modern. The container that holds these sedums and sempervivums (hens-and-chicks) was once several pieces of junk, rusting away in a salvage yard. They've been recycled into a container that mixes humor with a bold dash of style and works splendidly with this kitchen's contemporary stainless-steel countertop. Hunt through your attic, garage, or local salvage yard, and you'll find objects that can be converted into conversation pieces doubling as plant containers.

Since sedums and sempervivums are unaffected by any rust that leaches into their soil, you can plant directly into the weathered object of your choice, as long as it provides drainage and hasn't contained harmful chemicals in a previous life. Place the container where it will receive bright direct sun for most of the day. These are easy-to-grow plants that need little care as long as you don't overwater them.

Garden Miscellany

Sempervivum's name is Latin for "live forever," in reference to how easily the plant propagates itself. Sedum means "sit" or "hold fast," a nod to the plant's ability to attach to rocks, walls, and even rooftops.

Herb Trough

With a small herb garden

this close at hand, you may actually find yourself looking forward to the question "What's for dinner?". This stone trough of bay laurel, sweet basil, parsley, thyme, nasturtium, and variegated oregano will fill your kitchen with enticing aromas while ensuring fresh herbs are just a pinch away. The Mexican tile in this kitchen is a strong partner for the impressive-looking container.

Small potted herbs are easy to find these days; they may even be offered in your grocery's produce section. Pot your herbs directly into a container with good drainage, and then place the herb garden where it will receive at least four hours of direct sun each day. Herbs don't like to have wet feet, so allow the soil to dry out a bit between waterings. Herbs also respond poorly to overfeeding, so fertilize with an all-purpose fertilizer just enough to keep the plants healthy (once a month or less), but be careful not to overdo it. This particular group of herbs should last indoors for a couple of months; after that, it would be happy to summer outdoors on a deck or patio.

Garden Miscellany

To dry herbs, gather the stems together with a rubber band, and hang the bunch upside down in a dark location that's warm and dry. When the leaves feel papery and rigid, the herbs can be stored in a dark glass container with an airtight lid.

Miniature Gerber Daisy

A home for Thumbelina?

Miniature gerber daisies can often be found in grocery stores. Go ahead and put one in your shopping cart (it'll cost about the same as a box of cereal); this diminutive bloomer will charm you for weeks. You'll have fun moving this highly transportable plant from spot to perfect spot. Here, the flowers create a nice echo of the blossoms on the tray in the background, and the textured leaves work well with the textured braid on the table's edge.

We couldn't resist setting this one into a Japanese tea cup, but to help yours last as long as possible indoors (up to six weeks in ideal conditions), pot your miniature gerber into a small pot with good drainage. Gerber daisies also do best when they have lots of light with some direct sun, and evenly moist soil while blooming. (After blooming, they can be allowed to dry out slightly between waterings.) Cool temperatures will help ensure plenty of blooms; temperatures over 70°F (21°C) may cause them to stop blooming. They will also appreciate being fed every other week with a water-soluble fertilizer and an occasional misting of their leaves. Remove spent flowers to encourage more blooms.

Garden Miscellany

Here are some troubleshooting tips for gerber daisies: No blooms: Try giving your plant more light. Wilting: Plant may be too warm or too dry. Powdery mildew on leaves: Conditions are too cool and humid. Plants may be overcrowded or suffering from poor air-circulation (see page 22). Leaves turn black: Plant is too cold; move to a warmer location.

Corkscrew Rush

No, this plant isn't

having a bad hair day. It's corkscrew rush, a grasslike perennial that's found streamside in nature. Pot it into sand and soil-filled glass containers, and it will look sensational indoors. The containers' rectangular shapes and silver accents echo the architecture and stainless steel of this kitchen splendidly, while the rushes' wiry foliage adds a dramatic counterpoint to all those straight lines.

You'll find corkscrew rush at nurseries and home centers that sell plants for water gardens. These three rushes were simply placed in glass vases filled first with sand, then a paper coffee filter, and then potting soil. (A bit of Spanish moss was added to the containers' edges for decorative effect.) Placed in a location that receives direct or bright light, and with the soil kept continually moist, these arrangements would last for a couple of weeks indoors. If you pot them into slightly larger containers (the sand is merely decorative and isn't necessary) give them adequate light and water, and feed them with a weak dose of liquid fertilizer once a month, you may be able to keep them indoors longer.

Garden Miscellany

If you'd like to transplant these tangled masses of beauty to the outdoors, they can go directly into the ground beside a pond or into a bog garden. But you may want to keep them contained outdoors instead, as rush can be invasive.

Rosemary Heart Topiary

Rosemary is an easy herb to fall in love with. Grown on a sunny countertop or windowsill, it will add fragrance, flavor, and even flowers to your kitchen year-round. Rosemary has been used in topiary since ancient times. This one has been trained to a wire frame, but it can also be grown and pruned into a standard (a leafy globe atop a single stem—see page 65 for instructions) or shaped to resemble a miniature Christmas tree. The plant, pot, and counter surface all work together wonderfully in this kitchen.

Rosemary likes full sun—if you place it in a south- or west-facing window, it's more likely to bloom in winter. Allow the soil to dry out between waterings, but guard against letting the plant go completely dry for a long period, as it may not recover. Like most herbs, rosemary will be more fragrant and flavorful if grown in fairly poor soil, so don't bother with fertilizers.

Training rosemary to a frame is easy. Start with a plant (trailing varieties work best) with two long tendrils. Make the frame by bending a coat hanger or a piece of strong, flexible wire into the shape of a heart with a stem at the end. Insert the stem into the potting soil close to the plant, but be careful not to injure any roots. Gently twine the plant's branches up and around the frame, tying them loosely with raffia or strips of cloth. As the plant grows, continue to twine and tie new growth to the frame and prune any excess growth. Turn the rosemary regularly, to keep it from becoming lopsided.

Garden Miscellany

Rosemary has delicate lavender, blue, or pink flowers. If you're growing the herb more for culinary than decorative purposes, pinch off the blossoms—the oils in the leaves will be weaker when the plant is producing flowers.

Moss Containers

Are they plants or pets?

It's impossible to pass these velvety mounds of moss without stopping to give them a gentle pat. If you have a source of moss nearby, transforming small clumps into a striking conversation piece will take practically no time at all. The hammered metal containers (found in the toiletries section of a home decorating shop) make sophisticated, contemporary holders that turn the collection into a study of texture and form.

Moss plantings such as these should be considered temporary. Moss is difficult to grow indoors, and does better when placed in shallow containers. But this easily made display should last at least a couple of weeks, and then you can simply lift off the faded moss and replace it (many homeowners equate moss with mess, and are happy to part with whatever is growing in their yard).

Collect moss (always with permission) with a trowel, spatula, or large spoon, trying to leave as much soil as possible attached to the plant. (It will be harder to get moss that's growing on stone or wood to survive in a pot with soil.) Fill your containers with potting soil to which water-absorbent polymer crystals have been added. (Make sure the potting soil doesn't contain calcium, which kills moss.) Press the moss into the soil and water very slowly. Then place the moss in a location where it receives indirect light (fairly bright light, if it grew outdoors in sunlight; less bright, if it grew outdoors in the shade). Mist the moss every day and water as needed.

Garden Miscellany

Fossil records indicate that moss has grown on our planet for at least 400 million years. Today, over 15,000 species of moss cover Earth from the Arctic to Antarctica. While many homeowners consider it a nuisance, the Japanese have cultivated entire gardens of moss for centuries.

Indoor Salad Garden

Here's a whimsical

kitchen garden that looks good enough to eat, and it is! This colander of fresh salad greens and edible flowers is so attractive, you'll hate to harvest it, but deadheading the flowers and trimming the lettuce is just what's needed to keep this indoor garden growing. The colander makes a decorative container with holes that allow the soil to drain well and breathe. The handles make it a cinch to transport the entire garden to the kitchen sink at watering time.

Depending on the size of the holes in your colander, you can either pour good-quality potting soil directly into it, or first add the sort of liner made for hanging baskets. These are made from coir, coco-fiber, or even cardboard—just make certain the one you purchase is safe to use with edible plants. You'll have the best luck with this container garden if you start with lettuce seedlings from a nursery or garden center, rather than trying to sow seeds. Choose a couple of varieties of looseleaf lettuce that will keep growing when trimmed. The violas and pansies can also be purchased as seedlings; just make sure you buy organically raised flowers, so they'll be safe to eat. Simply plant the seedlings, water well, and set the colander in a cool spot where the plants will receive both bright light and protection from midday sun. Keep the colander well watered and fertilized with a weak dose of all-purpose fertilizer.

Garden Miscellany

Pansies and violas are high in both vitamin C and beta-carotene. The taste of pansies is similar to that of lettuce, while violas tend to have a mild wintergreen flavor. To be safe, always eat the petals only, and start with a small amount. People with allergies or asthma should not eat flowers.

Sedum in Silver

Want elegance without

a lot of fuss? Try sedum in a silver centerpiece bowl. This succulent looks like the kind of plant you'd have to be an expert to grow, but it's actually a hard one to kill. The glaucous blue-green foliage of trailing sedum (which is often tinged with pink or dusky purple) is the perfect match for just about any silver-toned container. The antique appearance of this bowl and the arresting form of the plant give this duo a refined drama that works wonderfully in this modern loft kitchen.

Outdoor gardeners are familiar with sedum (also called stonecrop) as a perennial valued for its late summer and fall color. But it also grows well indoors. If you're planting directly into a container (like the one shown) that doesn't have drainage holes, be sure to put a 1-inch (2.5 cm) layer of gravel or pot shards at the bottom, because sedum does need well-drained soil. The plant's color will be at its best if you can provide at least four hours of direct sun each day, but sedum can survive with less direct light. Allow the soil to dry out a bit between waterings. Most sedums will become semi-dormant in winter; water then only enough to keep the leaves from shriveling. Feed your plant just three times a year (in very early spring, late spring, and late summer) with a 10-20-10 fertilizer at half the recommended strength.

Garden Miscellany

Sedum has been grown since ancient times, and superstitions connected with the plant abound. Once called "midsummer men," sedum was used in various ways to predict love. In one custom, the plant was hung by a young woman on midsummer's eve. If the leaves bent to the right, that was a sign that her sweetheart was true. If they bent to the left, he was cold and faithless.

Cactus & Sedum Bowl

Color, form, and

texture figure boldly in this up-to-date composition. The tiny sedum and purple cactus have found the perfect home in this handmade earthenware bowl, and the bowl is the perfect complement to this bathroom vanity's rough countertop. You won't be able to find the identical container, but a little scouting at local craft fairs should uncover plenty of unique bowls to use instead (just be sure you'll be able to drill a hole in the bottom for drainage).

The sedum and cactus can be planted directly into any bowl that provides good drainage. An inch or two (2.5 to 5.1cm) of coarse gravel at the top of the potting soil will also ensure adequate drainage. Set the container where it will receive as much direct sun as possible. The soil for these plants should be allowed to dry out almost completely between waterings, especially in winter. If you place this combination in a bathroom that tends to stay humid, you'll need to water even less frequently.

Garden Miscellany

For painless cactus planting, wear thick gloves or use ice or barbecue tongs (or even newspaper folded into a thick strip) to pick up the prickly plant.

Hyacinths in a Row

Hyacinths in silver

cups is a simple way to add elegance, bold color, and heady fragrance to any room. Here, they accent the room's chrome towel racks and suit its contemporary style. One of the easiest of bulbs to force, the hyacinth has an intoxicating scent that brings a breath of spring months ahead of schedule. (You may want to leave them out of the dining room, so their aroma doesn't compete with the food.) Getting the color just right should be easy—the voluptuous flowers come in white, pink, red, lavender, purple, blue, apricot, and yellow.

The bulbs can be forced in soil or water (see page 31 for instructions) to flower as early as Christmas, or you can buy potted plants just about to bloom in grocery stores, gardening centers, and florist shops starting in January. Hyacinths will bloom for a few weeks if kept in a draft-free location with bright light, but not direct sun, and cool temperatures, especially in the evening. If your hyacinths are in the bathroom, and start to droop, set them in a cooler location while you bathe or shower. Because these plants like continually moist soil, proper drainage is important. To use a container such as these silver cups, which you certainly wouldn't want to drill holes in, place a layer of gravel in the bottom beneath the potting soil, or keep each hyacinth in its original pot, and use the decorative container as a cachepot. See page 33 for instructions on replanting bulbs out in the garden.

Gerber Daisies, Daffodils, Ferns & Violas

These daffodils, gerber daisies, violas, and ferns create a spring garden you can enjoy in the dead of winter. All of these plants were purchased at a grocery store (with the exception of the violas, bought at a gardening center) in the gray days of January. Line your container (in this case, a low wire basket) with a plastic saucer, and you can simply pop the plants, plastic grow pots and all, into the container, and then arrange Spanish moss to hide the grow pots.

These plants will do best in a cool location with bright, but not direct, light. Keep the soil in the pots evenly moist, and mist occasionally. This collection should last indoors for a couple of weeks if you can keep it cool enough (especially at night).

The ferns can be kept as houseplants indefinitely. Check with a local nursery (or local agricultural extension agency) to see whether the daffodils, violas, and gerber daisies will grow outdoors in your climate. If so, violas can be transplanted just about anytime; the daffodils and gerber daisies, after the last spring frost.

Garden Miscellany

Violas (also known as Johnny-jump-ups) are edible if they've been grown without pesticides. Use them to garnish a salad or decorate a cake—they're high in both vitamin C and beta-carotene.

Pansies in a Window

There's no denying

the elegance of a monochrome bathroom, but a splash of color can also be welcome. These bright orange pansies in their vintage metal container add a cheerful note without disrupting the serene atmosphere of the room. Because pansies can grow outdoors even in cold conditions, you can often find them for sale from late winter to late fall. They are almost always sold inexpensively as bedding plants and come in a great range of solid and three-tone colors.

Pansies are usually sold in plastic trays, so you'll want to remove them from the tray and plant them directly into a grow pot with good drainage (the grow pot could then be slipped into a cachepot). Place the pansies where they'll receive bright indirect light. Pansies will sulk if temperatures are too warm; if you set them directly in a window, make sure there's a blind or sheer curtain to protect them from midday sun. Keep the soil evenly moist, and deadhead spent blooms so the plants will continue blossoming.

Garden Miscellany

Plant pansies outdoors in well-drained soil where they'll receive at least six hours of sun each day. When their flowers fade, cut the plants back by one-third. These plants will bloom right through 15°F (-9°C) temperatures (blue and yellow cultivars tend to be hardiest).

Botanical Names

A

African violet........*Saintpaulia*

ageratum........*Ageratum houstonianum*

aster........*Aster*

B

basil........*Ocimum basilicum*

bay laurel........*Laurus noblis*

bear grass........*Xerophyllum tenax*

begonia........*Begonia*

bird's nest fern........*Asplenium nidus*

butterfly orchid........*Phalaenopsis*

C

caladium........*Caladium*

calla lily........*Zantedeschia*

canna lily........*Canna*

cape primrose........*Streptocarpus*

carex grass (or sedge)........*Carex*

cattail (dwarf)........*Typha minima*

Chinese painted fern........*Pteris tremula*

chrysanthemum........*Chrysanthemum weyrichii* (synonym: *Dendranthema weyrichii*)

coleus........*Solenostemon scutellariodes*

coral bells........*Heuchera*

corkscrew rush........*Juncus effusus* 'Spiralis'

creeping Jenny........*Lysimachia nummularia*

D

daffodil........*Narcissus*

G

gerber daisy........*Gerbera jamesonii*

H

hosta........*Hosta*

hyacinth........*Hyacinthus*

hydrangea........*Hydrangea macrophylla*

I

impatiens........*Impatiens*

ivy........*Hedera*

J

Japanese painted fern........*Athyrium niponicum*

jasmine........*Jasminum*

L

leatherleaf sedge........*Carex buchananii*

lily........*Lilium*

lily of the Nile........*Agapanthus*

M

mandevilla........*Mandevilla*

marigold........*Tagetes*

moth orchid........*Phalaenopsis*

mother fern........*Asplenium bulbiferum*

muscari (or grape hyacinth)........*Muscari*

myrtle........*Myrtus*

N

nasturtium........*Tropaeolum*

O

oregano........*Origanum vulgare*

P

pansy........*Viola wittrockiana*

parsley........*Petroselinum crispum*

passionflower vine........*Passiflora*

plumbago........*Ceratostigma plumbaginoides*

R

rose........*Rosa*

rosemary........*Rosmarinus*

S

sedum (or stonecrop)........*Sedum*

sempervivum (or hens and chicks)........*Sempervivum*

sweet potato vine........*Ipomoea batatas*

T

taro........*Colocasia*

thyme........*Thymus*

tulip........*Tulipa*

V

vinca........*Vinca*

viola........*Viola*